biography
B
GIBSON

92
Gib

Gibson, Althea

So much to live
for

5387

DATE			
JAN 5			
MAR 2 1 1997			
APR 1 5 1997			

5387

So Much to Live For

Althea Gibson tells her own story of what happened to her after she put away her tennis racket and decided to earn her keep as a professional golfer. She tells of the hard and grueling work to improve her game, of her few brushes with race prejudice, and of the people who helped and encouraged her. Miss Gibson faced many challenges and made some mistakes. But she feels the exhilaration of what she describes as "challenging again," as she sets her sights on the top honors in professional golf.

So Much to Live For

By Althea Gibson
with Richard Curtis

G. P. PUTNAM'S SONS, NEW YORK

To my husband, William
Who is most understanding in objectives
and sincere in thought.

Second Impression

Contents

Sports Shelf Biographies You Will Enjoy

Henry Aaron: Quiet Superstar
by Al Hirshberg

Sandy Koufax: Strikeout King
by Arnold Hano

Ted Williams
by Ray Robinson

My Ups and Downs in Baseball
by Orlando Cepeda and Charles Einstein

Roberto Clemente: Batting King
by Arnold Hano

Stan Musial: Baseball's Durable "Man"
by Ray Robinson

Willie Mays: Coast to Coast Giant
by Charles Einstein

Mickey Mantle: Mister Yankee
by Al Silverman

Ken Boyer
by David Lipman

The Johnny Unitas Story
by Lee Greene

Bob Cousy
by John Devaney

Jim Brown: The Running Back
by Larry Klein

So Much to Live For

Introduction

THE end of summer 1958 found Althea Gibson in a position most women would envy. She had not only climbed to the top of the amateur tennis world by winning the British and American world championships the year before, but had now proved she deserved them by successfully defending these crowns. The first Negro woman ever to hold such titles, she was now flushed with her triumph over Angela Mortimer at Wimbledon and Darlene Hard at Forest Hills. She had been honored with a ticker-tape parade by the city of New York, and *Time* magazine had featured her face on its cover—distinctions which have been conferred on the noblest personages of modern times. In January of 1958, 214 sports writers and broadcasters, casting their ballots in the Associated Press poll, had cited her Female Athlete of the Year, bestowing an overwhelming number of votes on her: 420 out of 516. As a result, she was awarded the Frederick C. Miller Award and the Babe Didrickson Zaharias Trophy.

Yes, she was definitely at the summit of her career. She had achieved everything she'd dreamed of achieving, everything that almost all women athletes dream of achieving.

So you'll probably be bewildered, as many people were then, to read the statement she made on September 7th of that year before the throng at Forest Hills, where she had moments earlier won the American crown for the second year in a row. The essence of it was as follows:

> I wish to announce my retirement from the ranks of amateur tennis players. I am tentatively setting a period of retirement at one year. That is to say, I am retiring from amateur competition as of this time for a period of at least one year.
>
> I am thirty-one years old, but in my opinion have reached my peak only within the last two years. Therefore, even though I retire for one or even two years, I will not stop practicing my tennis and will in all probability engage in exhibitions in order to maintain my touch.
>
> It is quite possible that at the end of my retirement I *may* return to tournament competition. . . .

My titles are now open to anyone who wins the tournaments I have won. This applies specifically to my titles at Wimbledon and Forest Hills, but is not limited to them.

The reaction to her decision was, naturally, great puzzlement, and a few spectators sitting in the stands that day, as I was, registered shock. Those of us who had followed her career closely knew, or thought we knew, that Althea Gibson had found the fulfillment of her ambitions. This action seemed totally contradictory to the values she had strived and sacrificed for.

Some years later, I took advantage of an opportunity to be introduced to her, and our conversation was a memorable one for me. She was now making headway in a new field of competition, professional golf, and I was forcefully impressed by her determination to reach the top. But the question that had disturbed me in 1958 was still unanswered. I told her about my response to her decision to retire and asked if she could shed some light on what had motivated her. Her answer, and the events of her life since 1958, inspired me with the idea for this book.

The biographical facts leading to her successful siege of the highest fortresses in tennis are generally well known. She was born on August 25, 1927, in Silver, South Carolina, daughter of a poor sharecropper who moved, while Althea was young, to New

York City. Harlem life was, in its way, as tough as the life the family had left, and Althea got into many scraps and scrapes. Had it not been for a Police Athletic League play-street program in which she was able to divert her hostility and energy into a constructive channel, she might very well have become a juvenile delinquent. As it was, she still got into lots of trouble.

Luckily Fred Johnson, then pro at the Cosmopolitan Tennis Club, having observed her skill in paddle tennis, encouraged her and gave her lessons. She excelled, and in 1942 the fifteen-year-old girl entered and won her first tournament, the girls' singles division of the New York State Open Championship, put on by the largely Negro American Tennis Association. In the following years she began to win consistently in A.T.A. competition, first in the national girls' division, then in the national women's. She had in 1946 received a big boost when Dr. Hubert A. Eaton and Dr. Robert W. Johnson arranged for her to be taken in by their families—Dr. Eaton's in Wilmington, North Carolina, during the school year and Dr. Johnson's in Lynchburg, Virginia, during the summer—in order for her to get her high school diploma and to free her from financial cares so that she could play tennis. This was a turning point. In 1947 she won every tournament she played in, including the A.T.A. women's singles, and she went on for the next nine years to win the latter championship. The year 1949 was especially important to her.

12

She graduated from high school—education has always been deeply important to her—was offered a scholarship at Florida A&M, and entered two United States Lawn Tennis Association tournaments, the first Negro woman to do so.

The story from there is one of constant growth, not without setbacks and heartaches. Between 1952 and 1955 she was never ranked higher—that is, worse—than 13th in U.S.L.T.A. standings. In 1955 she was honored by the U.S. State Department with an offer to represent this country with Ham Richardson, Bob Perry, and Karol Fageros in a goodwill tennis tour of Southeast Asia. It was an overwhelming success, and she returned ready to take her place on the international stage in tennis competition. In 1956 she won the French and other foreign championship matches, and suddenly she was talked about as America's most dynamic woman athlete. In 1957 she justified the speculation by beating Darlene Hard at Wimbledon, England and Louise Brough at Forest Hills, New York, to become both British and American—and therefore world—champion.

And that brings us to 1958 and the announcement of her retirement after her second Wimbledon and Forest Hills triumphs. Why would anyone in her shoes do it? Though the world of amateur tennis was packed with tough contenders, none of them was able enough to threaten her crown, nor would anyone be in that position for a long time to come. All she had to do was, in effect, guard her throne by playing tennis at least as well as she'd played in the last two years, and the future would be guaranteed. It was unlikely she would play worse; chances were far more likely she would get even better. "Then why?" was the question put to her a dozen times a day. And what has happened since then?

Here, in Althea Gibson's own words, is the moving story of those years.

RICHARD CURTIS

1

So Much to Live For

"BEING a champ is all well and good," I would tell the well-meaning people who asked me about my retirement, "but you can't eat a crown. Nor can you send the Internal Revenue Service a throne clipped to their tax forms. The landlord and grocer and tax collector are funny that way: they like cold cash. I may be the Queen of Tennis right now, but I reign over an empty bank account, and I'm not going to fill it by playing amateur tennis, even if I remain champ from now until Judgment Day."

Yes, I'm afraid the reason for my retirement was Old Devil Money.

I'm not, certainly, deriding the enormous spiritual satisfactions I got from my triumphs as an amateur. Few humans know the sweet joys of being congratulated personally by the Queen of England, or being presented with the medallion of the city of New York by its mayor after being snowed under with confetti and ticker tape in the canyons of Broadway, or simply feeling that swelling in your heart that comes with possession of the honors you've coveted since the first moment you swung a tennis racket.

But when the applause and the homage are over, the guests departed from the victory parties, the telegrams and flowers strewn about like the spoils of a military campaign, the bright trophies mounted in dazzling array on the mantle, you ask yourself what material things these satisfactions can buy. Then you feel like a host sitting among the debris of a fabulous party he's just thrown, and in his hands is a sheaf of bills. He may still be giddy with the effects of the fun and alcohol, but he knows that in the morning he's going to have a whopping headache and an army of troubles.

The truth, to put it bluntly, is that my finances were in heartbreaking shape. I had a few outside sources of money, but they were quite meager. I was prohibited from capitalizing on my tennis ability to make money; otherwise, I would be jeopardizing my amateur status. The allowances paid to me for expenses incurred on my tennis tours barely covered my outlays. In fact, as often as not, I exceeded the allowances and had to pay costs out of my own pocket. I was no spendthrift either, believe me, but the United States Lawn Tennis Association's budget restrictions were so severe that only the most frugal person could make ends meet. I had relied on the unstinting aid of two friends, Dr. H. A. Eaton of Wilmington, North Carolina, and Dr. R. W. Johnson of Lynchburg, Virginia. But their resources weren't unlimited, and, more important, my pride forbade me from accepting their assistance any longer. On the contrary, it was time I started repaying these dear men for their sacrifices.

In my travels around the world, I had had a chance to observe the comfortable way that many decent people lived. This exposure had touched me not with envy but certainly with a modest ambition to live as comfortably. I didn't aspire to luxury, but I did believe there was no reason why I, too, shouldn't have some of the good things that make life pleasant. Much has been said defending the virtues of poverty, but I've rarely met anyone who, if he was honest with himself, would choose it after seeing the benefits that come with having money.

I wasn't asking for something for nothing. I'd struggled and felt entitled to be rewarded for the struggle, and more significantly, I had won and felt entitled to rewards for winning. And just as important in my mind was the welfare of my parents, who had drudged

17

in poverty to raise me in a dangerous, grudging world and deserved a return on their investment of toil and heartache.

So as I progressed through 1958, I began to think of leaving amateur tennis for more profitable fields. It was a terribly difficult decision. There was so much I would have to give up, and I kept asking myself if I was being greedy in wanting money when others might settle for the less tangible prizes. But I finally forgave myself. I reasoned that if I *was* opting in favor of money, at least I wasn't alone—about a billion other humans do it every day.

That summer I stood at the crossroads and surveyed the paths I could take on leaving amateur tennis. Now that I've been down some of those paths and can look back over my shoulder, I realize that I underestimated the hazards ahead of me. I wasn't a child then, but my mistaken judgment was nevertheless the product of youthful inexperience, for I deceived myself that the important lessons in life lay behind me. It was my old nemesis, the swelled head, that led me into that error.

Most folks in my situation would never have stepped out of one status unless they had definite offers in negotiation or even had in their pockets signed contracts guaranteeing a minimum amount of money to be counted on for the next year or two. But I had no such guarantees in hand and had a very unclear idea of where I was going. I relied heavily on the fame I had achieved and on my faith in myself and in Providence to provide for the future. I have no deep regrets that I didn't look more carefully before I leaped, but if I had to do it again, I might ask Providence to "put it in writing."

What were the possibilities?

Well, first and foremost was professional tennis. There are four ways a professional tennis player can make money: he can become a teaching pro at a tennis or country club; he can go on tour with a group of players; he can enter specific tournaments and play for cash prizes; and he can promote products for a sponsor.

As for becoming a teaching pro, I frankly didn't weigh it too seriously. It meant retiring from competition to a degree that a person of my combative nature would find unbearable. Sure, I wanted to pass along to others the skills and techniques that had helped me win championships, but because I put my heart into everything I do, I knew that I would involve myself too deeply in the development of my pupils. I foresaw that my obligations to them would prevent me from engaging in many matches with players of top-flight ability. This would be disastrous. When a good player doesn't get an opportunity to pit his total skill and energy against a powerful opponent, he goes to seed.

19

Furthermore, it was somewhat unrealistic for me to consider becoming a pro at a club because there was the larger question of whether any clubs would consider *me*. Even if I'd had an unquenchable yearning to be a teaching pro, the clubs weren't exactly tripping over themselves to offer me jobs. It was here that the barrier of race slammed in front of my face. To hail my talents in public doesn't cost anything, but to hire a Negro—and a Negro woman at that—to teach white club members called for a bigger expenditure of courage than most club owners were willing to make. So by mutual consent the course of becoming a teaching pro was ruled out.

The second course, going on tour, was much more promising, and I'd been approached by a number of groups. There were only a few really big-money tennis tours such as Jack Kramer's—and Kramer's organization had not entered into negotiations with me—and unless I could join one of them on conditions which my coach, my attorney and I felt to be fair, I would have to discard the tour circuit, too. Smaller tours, such as there were, could not pay sufficiently to make it worthwhile. Touring from city to city is not the easiest way to make a living, so the pay has to be pretty good to compensate for the tedium and discomfort of travel. But as it eventually turned out, one of the tour offers did bear fruit, and the money and other conditions were attractive enough to lure me. I'll take this up in greater detail a few chapters on.

As a third alternative, I could enter matches and try to win cash purses, but there are really so few of these, and the awards so unglamorous, that it was impossible to make a living as what I suppose you would call a free lance. And the fourth alternative, endorsing and promoting products such as sporting goods, did not look too promising, either. I'd been receiving a small fee for advertising the products of one company, but none of the large firms wanted to pay me very much to endorse rackets or clothes or anything else.

In short, I had surprisingly few irons in the fire when it came to exploiting my tennis abilities in the professional field. But that doesn't mean there weren't other fires to put my irons into. On the contrary, I had never been completely convinced that my future lay in tennis. Even during the period when tennis had been my most absorbing concern, I was exploring some of my other abilities.

Some people are constituted in such a way that they can do one thing well and concentrate all their attention on developing that talent and that talent alone. But I'm afraid I'm not cast from that mold. I don't know if it's a blessing or a curse, but I'm flexible, and I believe in building on all the talents the Lord has endowed me with. And what's more, I have an abund-

21

ance of energy to spare for all these occupations and interests. So I try to be versatile. It's proven more of a help than a hindrance, because when I've found myself at the end of one road, I manage to start down a new one without fear. But there's such a thing as being too flexible, because you can dissipate your attention on so many vocations and avocations that you end up doing nothing well—a kind of athletic dilettante. I hoped to steer a course between the two extremes of behavior, keeping myself in condition in several fields but concentrating always on one course above all others.

Most important of all my alternatives was my singing career. As far back as 1943, when I'd won second prize in the amateur talent show held at Harlem's Apollo Theater, I had shown more than passing ability as a singer. In the fifteen years that followed, I was never without a melody on my lips.

I had the basic equipment to be a good singer: a strong but well-controlled voice, a fairly wide vocal range, and an individual style. What I lacked, however, was extensive training and guidance, and so in the fall of 1957 I set out to rectify that shortcoming. I went to work with James Scott Kennedy, a professor of speech and voice at Long Island University, toward eliminating the deficiencies in my delivery and accentuating the positive aspects of it. Unfortunately, the demands of tennis had taken me away from those studies, but now that tennis might not be consuming so much of my time I could, if I chose, involve myself more intensively in my voice lessons.

I had good reason to give serious thought to a singing career because 1957 and 1958 had given me some big breaks. I'd frequently been called on, while on the amateur tennis circuit, to sing before some pretty large audiences, and they had never failed to receive me with genuine enthusiasm. As a result, I was invited to sing at the gala testimonial dinner thrown at New York's Waldorf-Astoria in honor of W. C. Handy, the immortal creator of some of our greatest blues songs. My appearance there impressed an executive of Dot Records, who asked me if I wanted to cut a long-playing album for him. I joyfully accepted, and in the spring of 1958, my album was released. Even more significantly, Ed Sullivan asked me to appear on his television show around the time the record was released, to sing one of the songs on it. The song was "So Much to Live For," a title which summed up the way I felt at the time—which is why I've used it to head both this book and the opening chapter. I'll tell you more about these developments later on, but suffice it to say for now that they gave me keen hope that I could go far with my singing career if I decided to work on it with my customary energy.

At the same time, my theatrical agents were negotiating with some Hollywood studios on movie roles. I had never acted professionally, but evidently there were people who believed I had the raw material to be an actress. If a contract came out of the negotiations and I did well in a movie, it would lead to other offers and appearances. And who knows where I might go from there? I indulged in a few dreams of standing before an audience packed with glittering celebrities, humbly accepting the Oscar for my touching perform-ance in . . . As a matter of fact, as you'll see, a movie contract did pan out, but I'm afraid my fantasy was slightly overoptimistic. Well, at least it will show you the scope of my ambitions. I didn't want to do any-thing unless I truly believed I could do it better than anyone else. Set it down to egotism if you will, but I felt that if I threw myself into an acting career, an Academy Award for Best Actress was the least I would settle for before relaxing my relentless pace. No, that's not quite true; I would accept an Oscar for Best Sup-porting Actress.

My success story had interested a number of writers and publishers in the possibility of a book, and finally Ed Fitzgerald, the outstanding sports writer, and I set down the events of my life up to early 1958. Later in the year the book was published with the title *I Always Wanted to Be Someone*. It was greeted quite sympathetically and did much to help me convey to a wide audience some impression of the hardships I had endured, the joys I had experienced, and the outlook on life I had developed. I don't think the world is hanging on my lips for golden words of wisdom, but I do think the events of my life, and the viewpoint I've derived from them, are stimulating enough to inspire some readers to follow my good examples and shun my bad ones. And so much has happened to me since my first book was published that I feel I have to share these new experiences.

And last of all, there was golf.

Although years were to go by before I acted on it, I had the conviction as early as 1958 that that's where the future might hold its richest promise. There was hardly a sport that I hadn't tried at one time or another, if for no other reason than kicks. Golf was one in which I had shown a high degree of natural ability. With no coaching whatsoever, I could drive a golf ball way over 200 yards, and those who had observed my swing said that if I could harness my strength and adjust my attitude, I might in due time be in the same position in the golfing world as I was now in the world of tennis. By adjusting my attitude, I mean shifting from competition with other players to competition with myself, for golf is a constant fight with your own muscles for control.

The prospect in golf was compelling. No Negro woman had ever played, on any great scale, in the ranks of professional golfers. So, of course, no Negro woman had ever won a national or international pro golf tournament. And no woman, Negro or otherwise, had ever won championships in both tennis and golf.

The siren song of golf was barely audible to me when I retired from amateur tennis. But it was never completely out of hearing, and soon it was to grow so loud that I would not be able to resist its seductiveness.

You can see, then, that although I had no specific line of work in mind when I retired from amateur tennis, I had so many prospects on the horizon that the future held no anxiety for me at all. And the immediate future bore out my faith; it was filled with exciting and profitable activity. But beyond the horizon a few clouds had begun to boil, and the breezes from that direction, if I wanted to put my snoot into the wind, hinted that squalls could develop and develop fast. When life looks cheeriest, that's the time to be cautious, if not downright pessimistic. But I don't think that's the kind of wisdom young people are famous for heeding. And besides, I was indulging the delicious sensation of dreams come true, a sensation so nourishing that there were moments when I didn't care what unpleasantness the future might hold in store for me.

If I've given the impression that I was leaving amateur tennis because of disappointment in my accomplishments to date, or that I bore resentment against the world for not doing more for me than it had, I want to set the record straight here. It was with the

26

greatest sorrow that I made my departure from amateur tennis. If there had been any method at all for making ends meet and remaining in the game, I would have pursued it. But there wasn't, and because I wanted to make absolutely certain that my motives were pure, I turned the matter over in my mind as if inspecting a rare gem for flaws. It was too big a purchase to be ruined by trifling reasons.

Perhaps the best way to express how agonizing my decision was would be to quote the closing passage of my retirement announcement:

I cannot make this statement without thanking everyone, as well as the game of tennis itself, for what it has done for me. In particular I should like to open my heart to all the people in the tennis world, the members of the press, the people who have offered me advice and criticism on my game, and my friends, all of whom collectively made it possible for me to become women's champion of the world with their encouragement during the dismal days, understanding when all was not going as well as I had hoped, being patient when I myself became impatient. There are so many individuals and organizations, much too numerous to mention now, but they all know who they are. In all of this, I hope that I have accomplished just one thing: that I have been a credit to tennis and my country.

2

Starring Althea Gibson

AS I say, my singing stint at the Handy dinner led to my making a record album for Dot Records. I was thrilled with the opportunity and hoped it would lead to offers of theatrical and nightclub appearances and even to television. All through the winter of 1957 I worked on my style under the rigorous but patient tutorship of Professor Kennedy. The good professor came to like me and wrote the song I mentioned, "So Much to Live For," just for me.

There are countless numbers of wonderful tunes that describe passing moods, joy or sorrow, hope or despair, but I believe that every person has a unique theme that describes him basically, identifies him no matter what his mood may be. It's "his" or "her" song in the same way that couples in love have "our" song.

And if any phrase conveys my attitude toward life, no matter what setbacks I undergo, it's "So Much to Live For." I think Professor Kennedy shrewdly assessed my character when he wrote that song for me. It became not only my theme song but the theme of my life. And it was especially appropriate for that period in my life, for as I beheld the future, its promise was almost unbearably exciting.

Early in 1958 a date was set for me to record my album. Unfortunately, the schedule had a short fuse. You see, it's often difficult to get the right combo, the right singer, and the rest of the personnel together for cutting a record because they all have obligations to meet under their various contracts. Your combo may be booked for a gig in Detroit at just the time you become free to make your record; then, when your combo is through in Detroit and is ready to accompany you on the record, you have to go to St. Louis for a singing appearance.

So everybody is constantly scrambling around to be at the same place at the same time, and there's frequently little notice given of the moment when you and they will be able to gather under one roof long enough to record your album. That happened with me, and when the session was finally scheduled, only a week remained. I hastily selected my songs, but seven days left me little time to polish them, let alone rehearse them thoroughly with my group. What was worse, a few days before the session I came down with the flu. The big day couldn't be postponed, and so I had to climb out of a sickbed to perform.

If you've ever tried singing with a chest cold, you know it sounds something like a cow mooing into a megaphone, so I wasn't exactly in top condition to launch the voice that would eclipse Ella Fitzgerald's and Peggy Lee's overnight.

Still, swaddled in heavy sweaters and pumped full of tea and lemon and medicine, I managed to restore my voice to something like its usual quality. The songs I'd selected were eleven standards, like "I Can't Give You Anything But Love," "Don't Say No," and "I'm Just a Prisoner of Love," plus "So Much to Live For."

I was accompanied by the Doles Dickens Quartet, consisting of piano, guitar, bass and drums, and they followed me beautifully, considering the little time we'd had to work together. But as if conditions weren't bad enough, I had to record the entire album in one sitting, and that's a grueling experience even for a star who's been making records for years. I don't like to make excuses for myself, but I have to say that conditions were far from ideal. Nevertheless I did my best, and the finished product, under the circumstances, wasn't displeasing to the ear.

The producers of the Ed Sullivan Show heard about

my forthcoming record, which was to be released in May of that year, 1958. They asked me if I'd like to appear on the show during the week of release so that I could plug it, and you can be sure my answer wasn't no. On the contrary, between the time of their invitation and the time of my appearance, I was chirping like a bird.

I selected *my* song, "So Much to Live For," for that appearance, and this time I was in good health. Ed Sullivan was extremely cordial and the audience most warm. I was keyed up like an overwound watch but managed to relax myself before going on with the kind of self-administered pep talk I'm used to giving myself before tennis matches.

I'm told that to the average viewer at home my performance gave the impression of what the recording industry calls a "bad mix." That is, there was poor balance between the orchestra and my voice, and I was somewhat overpowered by the musicians. Be that as it may, I was in good form that evening, and the audience received me with a very big round of applause.

This good response, plus my tennis triumphs later in 1958, caused Ed to invite me back for a second appearance. On that occasion I did "I Should Care," orchestrated for me by Luther Henderson, and once again the audience gave me a big hand.

In spite of my gratitude to Ed Sullivan and my gratification over the applause, I've always had some uneasiness over the genuineness of the enthusiasm for my singing which was displayed on those two occasions. It was important to me that my singing be accepted for the right reason, that is, simply because it was good, and not because it was novel that a champion tennis player could also sing. I sometimes wonder what would have happened if I'd been introduced not by the name Althea Gibson but under some pseudonym so that the audience (assuming it was unfamiliar with my face) had to judge me strictly on the basis of what it heard. But perhaps I'm being too self-critical. Ed Sullivan is a shrewd judge of talent and a good showman. He has too much prestige to protect to take the risk of inviting a poor singer onto his show just because she's big in some other field. Look at it this way: anyone who's heard athletes singing in a locker room knows it's a long, long way between the shower stall and the stage or studio. So I'm confident that Ed Sullivan believed in me when he invited me to appear on his show. And if there was doubt in my mind about the purity of the producers' motives that first time, it was all but dispelled when they invited me for a reprieve later that year.

At the time of my first Sullivan appearance, the record was released with the title *Althea Gibson Sings.*

Whether it was due to the poor conditions under which I'd made the record, to the reluctance of people to try something new, or to cynical doubt about the talent of a singing tennis player or weak promotion, the record did not live up to my expectations. In fact, it sank beneath a sea of indifference.

Naturally, this disappointment saddened me, but I can't say it shattered my singing career. I was optimistic that I would get other chances to prove my vocal ability and would one day have an opportunity to make a record with more preparation, better training, and under better circumstances. Meanwhile, though, I had something else in the works which commanded so much of my interest that I couldn't afford the luxury of feeling sorry for myself.

I was going to be in a Hollywood movie.

The Mirisch Company had expressed interest in me, and my agents had managed to persuade them that in spite of my lack of formal dramatic training I had stage presence, natural acting ability and whatever else it took to be convincing on the screen. I suspect that my agents' vigorous enthusiasm for me was colored by their appetite for a commission—agents will be agents, after all. But I found their support so flattering and the prospect of a high salary so compelling that it wasn't difficult for me to restrain myself from modestly repudiating my agents' praise. Mirisch had a role in a movie that they thought would be an ideal vehicle for me, and so I signed a contract for an extremely handsome sum of money.

The film was to be called *The Horse Soldiers,* a Civil War movie set in Vicksburg, Mississippi—perhaps you've seen it in the theaters or on television. John Ford had been chosen to direct it, and it was to star John Wayne, William Holden, and Connie Towers. To a movie addict like me, it was impossible to repress a kind of bobby-soxer giddiness at the thought of appearing in the same movie with these idols, and though I may be graceful on the tennis court, I felt, the first time I met them, as if I were stepping on my own hands. But they were as charming in person as they were on the screen, and they put me completely at ease.

The part for which I was cast was that of maid and companion to the heroine, a Southern belle. I knew more about that kind of life than anyone on the set guessed, being the daughter of a Southern sharecropper. But while I went along with wearing the authentic costume of that period, right up to the handkerchief on my head, I drew the line at some of the dialogue they put into my mouth. The script called for a grossly heavy Negro dialect replete with "Yassuh's" and "Yassm's," and I found these offensive and unnecessary. Furthermore, they were unnatural to me.

35

I felt I could deliver the dialogue in my own style without betraying the intention of the writers or stepping out of character.

So Althea Gibson did the prima donna bit.

Actually it was a very minor dispute, and though I would have liked to storm off the set and retreat to a mountain hideaway to sulk until the producers begged me to return, I did nothing so histrionic. But though my protest was quiet, I was resolutely determined not to utter lines that reflected so negatively and distortedly the character of a colored woman. I felt that my own dignity and the dignity of the American Negro were on the line, and though I realized I was jeopardizing that delicious salary for the sake of a principle, I was prepared to act to that length if necessary to illustrate my sincerity.

When the powers that be recognized that I meant what I said, they conceded the point and deleted the obnoxious lines.

The mere thought of being on the set of a Hollywood movie was almost as stimulating as the anticipation of acting in the film itself, and I hung around the studio for the thrill of looking and listening, touching and smelling an atmosphere which had been as occult to me as the inside of an Asiatic monastery. Most of the personnel took it for granted, but for me it was deeply satisfying even to trip over a cable or bump my head on a boom. On those days when I was not involved in a scene, I'd show up anyway, just to watch the action and observe the incredibly complex technical and human elements that blend to make the refined product you see on the screen. On days when they *were* shooting a scene with me in it, I was required to show up on the lot at seven in the morning, a perfectly obscene hour to be doing anything but hitting the pillow as far as I'm concerned. But I loved Hollywood so much I would bounce in at seven, groggy but ready to involve myself in whatever there was to do, even if it was but to sit still and keep my mouth shut. Throughout the filming I was never sure if it was stardust in my eyes or just plain exhaustion.

Frequently I'd be scheduled for a scene only to learn, when I got on the set, that some delay or another required a postponement. It was frustrating, but John Ford was so kind and tactful, and the other actors so solicitous, that I accepted this state of affairs without complaint. If you could have witnessed the confusion, you'd have wondered how they managed to make one scene, let alone a whole movie. Though most of the goings-on were opaque to me and to many other individuals there, I believe the director had the whole scheme in his head, and we went along with delays and foul-ups as if they, too, were part of his plan.

John Ford is a marvelous man as well as a mar-

37

velous director. He helped imbue the set with a family atmosphere, so that the actors and technical people gave freely of themselves out of devotion to him, rather than working strictly for the money or because some tyrant ordered them around. I have always believed that love is the most potent force on earth, and it was with love that Ford treated us. He would sit down with everyone involved in a scene and try to inspire him with the spirit of the lines, so that instead of mouthing dialogue we felt we were fitting another link into the chain he was forging. He was most erudite, and we were treated to lessons in American history, weapons, costumes and other subjects that filled us with awe for his seemingly limitless acquaintance with the material of which his movies were made. He took great pains with me, knowing that my lack of training required him to pay special attention to details which were second nature to most professional actors.

And I must say his efforts were successful because I believe I did capture the essence of my part, and when I saw the completed film, I became so absorbed that I almost forgot that that was *me* up there. I appeared in six or seven scenes, and only one had been edited—or "left on the cutting-room floor," as we movie stars like to say—out of the rushes, the rough assembly of filmed scenes put together to give a general idea of the movie's quality.

At the end of the filming we threw a cocktail party, and I had the pleasure of hobnobbing with many actors and actresses I had always worshiped, including none other than Gregory Peck. It wasn't easy to keep the cocktail from shaking out of my glass.

That Christmas, back in New York City, a couple of gifts lay under my tree which I especially cherished. One was a flower-laden brandy snifter from William Holden. The other was a coffee mug sent by the "Duke" —John Wayne. On it was the following inscription:

ALTHEA GIBSON

THE HORSE SOLDIERS

TALLY HO

3

Althea Gibson, Businesswoman

THE HORSE SOLDIERS was released in the spring of 1959. Though it won no Academy Awards, it was many notches better than routine horse operas and was quite well received as a powerful portrayal of Southern life in that bitter era of American history. I was quite satisfied with my performance in it, and people whose judgment I respected said that I had a future in films. Unfortunately, the future isn't always dictated by people whose judgment you respect. My hopes that the motion picture would encourage producers to employ my talents further were dashed, for although my phone was ringing perpetually that spring, it bore no news of further film offers.

I took the disappointment philosophically, realizing that I hadn't really given the movie time to generate interest. Frequently one event can lead to another by such devious and casual means that it could take months or even years before my appearance in one movie influenced a producer to hire me for another. I don't feel it's for me to understand how the Lord works His wonders; I just try to work my own as far as they are in my power, and hope that Somebody up there is keeping my card in His active files.

Besides, by the time the movie was released, I had such a hot iron in the fire that I could afford to be a bit nonchalant about setbacks in my singing and acting careers. I was involved in earnest negotiations with the management of the Harlem Globetrotters.

I know what you're thinking, but don't get me wrong. I hadn't lost my mind and decided to abandon tennis for the life of a basketball player. Though I was sometimes to wonder if I didn't have what it took to play for the Globetrotters, I never had any serious intention of joining them in that capacity. If for no other reason than the problem of where to change my duds in their locker room, the idea presented just too many obstacles.

No, I had something entirely different in mind. The scheme was for me to organize a tennis tour of my own. That tour would join the Globetrotter itinerary, and before every Trotter basketball game, I would play a tennis match either with a local pro or with a permanent member of the tour. As you know, the

Globetrotters were and continue to be a tremendous box-office magnet, and so an awful lot of money was being talked about. I felt deeply honored to have offered to me a chance to be associated with a troupe that had done so much for basketball, for the Negro race, for sports in general, for the image of America overseas, and for the cause of brotherhood. I was definitely interested in the proposition and eager to go ahead with the tour if it could be made financially feasible.

I was no babe in the woods when it came to handling finances, but neither was I a captain of industry. Much of my experience handling money had to do with managing the modest funds at my disposal on amateur tennis tours. Considering the wee amounts I was given, and setting them against the ever-present temptation to blow them on one pretty dress or a fancy dinner, I have to congratulate myself on the admirable way I controlled my money. But the fact that you're clever at stretching a dollar doesn't guarantee that you'll be able to avoid the thousand pitfalls and snares that confront you when someone invites you to sign a contract with terms totaling five and maybe six digits. The only five-digit sums I'd ever earned, aside from my movie salary, had a decimal point in front of the last two digits.

Luckily, however, I was far from alone in my negotiations. I don't wish to sound cynical, but it's a fact of life that talented people on their way up attract large numbers of enterprising folks who are more than delighted to assist them in the handling and disbursement of their money—for a fee, of course, or a commission. I had not been exempt from that state of affairs, for as soon as I began winning championships in tennis and flirting with the idea of turning my talents in that and other fields into profitable avenues, I found myself with more advisers than Job. And many of them had advice as distasteful as the advice poor Job was given, too.

But the idea of putting my money affairs on a more businesslike basis was fundamentally a sound one, and so with the help of my coach I selected an attorney to represent me. The three of us then formed a corporation, Althea Gibson Enterprises. This company had come into existence the year before—1958, that is— and had been instrumental in working out my recording, television, book and movie contracts. The corporation of course was a closed one, meaning that you couldn't have called your broker and bought a share of stock in me if you'd been so inclined at the time. The three of us were to bear all the expenses and, if the Good Lord were willing, to reap all the profits of enterprises in which I got involved.

If the notion of an athlete organizing a business corporation to handle her operation horrifies you, let me assert that it is in reality the wisest thing a successful athlete can do. The point is important enough for me to digress for a moment and explain at length.

As you begin to make a name for yourself and the prospects of continued success become more and more likely, you're bound to be approached with a variety of business propositions. Many of these are unfeasible, and some of them are, I often think, the products of deranged minds. Others, however, are sound, sensible and potentially profitable. But whatever their nature, they require, at the very least, the courtesy of a reply. And looking at it more realistically, they usually require a good deal of time to look into their nature in some detail and, if they are basically agreeable, to thrash out terms.

After a little while of this, the chances are you'll be so beset with business decisions that unless they satisfy some secret urge in you to own a seat on the stock exchange, you'll begin to grow restless. You'll start craving the good old days when your only worries were to beat your opponents and not starve to death in the process. For now, on the other side of the net, is a host of opponents with such bewildering names as Guaranteed Annual Salary, Indemnity Provision, Promotional Budget, Escalation of Royalties, Whereby, Wherefore, Whereas, and Aforesaid!

Such complications are the certain result of success in this world. And whether you fully grasped the implications that first time you realized that you might, just might, one day be Number One in your field, business responsibilities are part of the bargain of being Number One. You can't be so frivolous as to turn back and revert to the days of innocent amateurism. So, with the conscientiousness of a good athlete, you say to yourself, "Well, as long as I've got to play this game, I might as well play it to win." And a sure way to win in the business game, or at least to make the most of your gains and the least of your losses, is to bring in competent professional help. Such people can give you authoritative aid in making the right decisions, in explaining the meaning of obscure contractual language, in comparing the deals you're offered with deals in which your fellow athletes are involved, and in pointing out to your untrained eye possible good or bad consequences of contractual terms.

So at the minimum you need a lawyer, but it's likely you'll need an accountant, too. If they have your best interests truly at heart, they'll certainly point out ways in which you can save on taxes, write off expenses legitimately, systematize your savings, invest your profits, or defer your earnings over a period of years to provide against a downturn in your fortunes. One good way to do all these things is to form a corporation.

Most people think that a corporation has to be the size of General Motors or Radio Corporation of America, but actually one person can incorporate himself and take advantage of certain benefits which the law extends to corporations. So if, when I said I formed one, you envisioned a sprawling trust with resources in the tens of millions, I have to say—it should only happen to me!

So you see, then, that my main reason for forming my company was to regularize my many business affairs and free myself to spend as much time as possible doing the very things on which the company depended for its profit: playing tennis, singing and acting, and so forth. This may seem ridiculously simple, but more than one athlete or entertainer has become so enmeshed in the web of his business affairs that he had to neglect or even abandon his career to attend to them. Arnold Palmer, who is certainly one of the best examples of an athlete corporation who through brilliant management has become a millionaire many times over, has expressed that very fear, and perhaps one of his motives for selling some of his interests to the National Broadcasting Company was the desire to simplify his life. I don't pretend to know, but I imagine that if I were in his position, I'd be worried about smothering in an avalanche of paper work. But, I repeat, if any corporations are thinking of trying to smother me as Palmer is smothered, they aren't to interpret the above as a discouragement.

Anyway, a desire for order was my principal reason for forming a corporation, but I did have one other motive, a motive which had been conceived a long time before I'd made it to the top of the tennis world.

You see, I had given a lot of thought to the many inequities and hardships facing the struggling young athlete. I myself had suffered many of them personally or had watched them befall others, some of whom were very dear to me. I'm not talking by any means about racial discrimination only, though that certainly was high on the list. I'm also referring to such things as lack of money, training, facilities, opportunity, and lack of encouragement by eminent athletes in their field. With each incident I experienced or witnessed, I would say to myself, "If I'm ever in a position to do anything about this, I'm going to take measures to see to it that the next generation doesn't have to go through it."

And now, when I *was* in a position to be listened to and to influence people to listen to me, I began wondering how I could put my vows into action. It dawned on me slowly that I might form a tennis academy, or an even larger academy devoted to a variety of sports, to which young people from anywhere in the country, anywhere in the world, could come. To whatever degree they had money, they would pay their own way, but if they were underprivileged, my academy would subsidize them.

Not only would these youths be trained and encouraged, but the school would bring their promising talents to the attention of amateur or professional sports organizations so that we would serve as a jumping-off place for "graduates." Not only would we teach sports themselves, but we would try to imbue the young athletes with the virtues of sportsmanship and mental and physical hygiene. We'd also try to instill a little business sense to help them look after themselves if and when they had an opportunity to convert their abilities into cash.

It was also my desire to do something about getting professional and amateur tennis players to mix. There is at present no pro-amateur tennis tournament, and each class is excluded from the other. But I believe that a great deal could be accomplished for the sport if promising amateurs could be permitted to compete against pros in certain tournaments or at least be allowed to play side by side with them in doubles tournaments. Toward this end I would work if I had a school of my own.

This dream of mine was as intense as anything I've ever wished for, and when the prospect of having money became more than a pipe dream, I started to sketch in my head the broad outlines of the Althea Gibson Academy. The formation of my corporation had been a first step toward the eventual philanthropic use of money I earned from my talents. I was not, of course, so naïve as to think that as soon as I had my hands on a few dollars, I would give them to one or two young and promising athletes, and that would be the extent of my contribution. No, my dream was a grand one, and it required money on a fairly grand scale, until which time Number One would have to be looked after. The Ford and Rockefeller and similar foundations had been made possible only after the founders' profit motive had been satisfied. In the same way, before indulging in the charitable act of spending money, I had to engage in the not-so-charitable act of earning some. The Globetrotter tour now presented a gleaming opportunity to do just that.

The bargaining and discussions of the tour's setup carried on into the summer, but both parties were genuinely interested in reaching a mutually amiable arrangement. These negotiations were considerably lubricated by the sincerity and goodwill of the Globetrotters' manager and owner, Abe Saperstein.

Abe was a man of rare qualities who demonstrated that love and business are not necessarily in conflict with each other. He loved sports, he loved his players, he loved the crowds, and he even loved his competitors and opponents. But he also loved money, or at least respected it, and all that love in his heart didn't make him a patsy at the bargaining table. He knew how to look after his boys' interests as well as his own, but he wasn't greedy and tried to make sure that everyone who dealt with him got a fair shake. He knew that the promoter's living depends on the happiness of his athletes, and the tales of his sacrifices for the sake of his players and friends are too numerous to list. This was a man I would be proud to work for, because he understood both athletes and money but knew that if he ever had to make a choice, it would be for athletes without a second thought. His death not long ago impoverished the world of sports.

But at this time his smiling eyes were alive and warm, and when we finally shook hands on our deal, I felt I'd been treated with eminent fairness. We put our pens to a document that would pay me more than any tennis player, man or woman, had ever been guaranteed. Though the money wasn't by any means free of expenses, it still represented a breathtaking sum to me —in the area of $80,000 to $100,000—of which I might be able to salt away a good deal if I handled my money economically.

As we finally decided, my corporation was to form a second corporation, which would have no other function than to handle matters connected with the Globetrotter tour. I was to form a road company which would appear with but still be independent of the Globetrotters. By this I mean that we would not travel in their bus or necessarily reside in the same hotels. We would have our own means of transportation and would have to arrange for our own accommodations in the towns and cities where the tour was to appear. We would have to foot all the expenses involved in these accommodations.

This was convenient both to the Trotters and to us because it left us free to keep our own schedule, while the basketball players could adhere to theirs. The Globetrotters were, to a man, gentlemen and sportsmen, but it would have been stretching their patience unnecessarily to ask them to hold up their bus a half hour while a lady adjusted the hem of her slip.

In spite of these independent arrangements, my tour was to be billed as a special attraction of the Globetrotter games. I was to select another female tennis player to accompany me on the tour, and we would play a set before each basketball game, or perhaps during half time. The tennis court would be set up on the basketball court or gymnasium floor, with base lines laid down with white tape and a portable net erected which could be knocked down speedily to permit the basketball team to get on the court for warm-ups without undue delay. These housekeeping functions were performed by my manager and his assistant doubling as roustabouts, and they got almost as much exercise from setting up the court as we did from playing on it. They jokingly suggested that since the audiences often applauded them as they scuttled around the floor laying tape, they should be billed with us as a feature of the program.

The conditions from one court to another were to

prove amazingly inconsistent. The lighting was not always brilliant, to say the least, and it gave the ball a shadow that caused it to play funny tricks on the eyes. And if you lobbed a ball high enough, you could lose it in the lights. And I mean that literally. On a few occasions the ball never came down, and the audience roared with laughter as I stood there, racket poised for a murderous slam, while the ball dribbled to rest on a rafter.

We recruited schoolboys to act as ball boys, and they did as well as could be expected. The virtue of a ball boy is that he maintains absolute stillness while volleys are in progress, even if it means freezing in an unnatural position. But untrained schoolboys are restless, and there were more than a few instances of one of these well-intentioned young men scampering in front of the net just as one of us was about to serve. A tennis player can pull a muscle interrupting his service, but more often the boys were the victims, and some of them, as souvenirs of their debuts as ball boys, brought home flaming red marks on choice parts of their anatomies.

For officials we frequently resorted to prominent businessmen or city officials from the town we were visiting at the time. Many of these gentlemen were as excited as schoolboys, for it was an honor for them to adjudicate our matches, and it satisfied that armchair daydream to get out in the center of a sports event and have thousands of people hanging on their decisions for the outcome. Their calls were usually fair, but on occasion they could be exasperatingly wrong, and even though my matches were exhibitions played in fun and not geared for winning titles, that didn't stop me from getting excited when an obviously bad call was made. Something happened to a few men when they found themselves holding so much power, and I wouldn't have been surprised if one or two had tried to order me off the court, fine me for bad conduct after I grumbled, and suspend me until some commission could review my case. But for the most part, these matches were quite enjoyable, and the amateur officials, giving and taking a lot of good-natured teasing, helped to make the events successful.

But what contributed above all to their success was the beauty and charm of my opponent and the rather astonishing costumes she wore.

4

On Tour

I HAD played against Karol Fageros in the early 1950's and found her as friendly and kindhearted as she was beautiful. But we really became close friends on the Southeast Asia tour in 1955 sponsored by the U.S. State Department. Afterward we faced each other as antagonists for the amateur titles. Although I played to beat her, it always broke my heart a little when I did —and I'm afraid I defeated her fairly consistently. It broke the hearts of many men in the galleries, too, because they loved to watch her graceful figure and wanted her to make her way up to the finals if for no other reason than to prolong the pleasure of seeing her perform. Because of the many thrilling experiences we had shared on our Asia trip, Karol and I had kept in close touch after my retirement from amateur tennis.

She was always uppermost in my thoughts whenever I considered my sports academy or a professional tennis tour.

And so when I had to decide whom I would like to have with me on the Globetrotter tour, I didn't hesitate in naming Karol. Happily she accepted my offer, and we two stalwart girl friends embarked on our expedition into the heartland of the United States.

Karol had been Florida State Junior Champion at the age of twelve and, mixing tennis talent with beauty even in her tender years, had been named Playground Queen at the age of fourteen. She had continued to work hard at her tennis and made respectable headway for herself in amateur ranks. Unfortunately, she never won any major titles, but she beat some of the best players in the game, including Louise Brough in 1956 and Angela Mortimer at Wimbledon in 1957. In 1957, in fact, she was ranked sixth in the world and fifth in the United States.

With improvement of her game went improvement of her beauty. In that competition she ranked with anyone going, displaying a figure of 36-25-36 at the age of twenty-five, when she joined the Globetrotter tour. Her hair was honey blond, because of which she'd been known as the Golden Goddess since her teen-age days. Capitalizing on her nickname, she had done something in 1958 that gave the tennis world something to talk about.

She had walked out on a tennis court wearing gold lamé panties.

Of course, flashy lingerie had become fashionable ever since Gussie Moran, earlier in the 1950's, had walked out on a court wearing pink lace panties under her skirt. But pink lace was as conservative as burlap compared to the shimmering undergarment Karol donned. According to her, the idea was suggested by actor Hugh O'Brian, whom Karol was dating at the time. The reception to her clothing was so gratifying— though no doubt most of the votes came from males— that gold lamé panties became her trademark, and the Golden Goddess came to be known by another alias: the Golden Panty Girl. So from then on she wore her eyecatching lingerie, and if you don't think that was expensive, think again. The gold in them thar pants priced them at $25 a pair, or roughly $1 a karat. It was a shame to see her sit down in them! For our tour she ordered forty-four more pairs, paying the sum of $1,100 for them, so you can see that this was no one-time gimmick.

And so, with Karol's bottom sheathed in gold lamé and mine in conventional white linen, we began barnstorming the country.

Our entourage consisted of Karol and myself, my secretary, our manager and his assistant. We bought a big station wagon with a U-Haul trailer, but even the trailer didn't carry all the stuff we had with us. So we had to pack the station wagon with five people, some of their luggage and equipment, and still make room for some semblance of a bed so that we could spell each other, napping between cities. The tour began officially in San Antonio, Texas, on November 17, 1959, and we were to cover the length and breadth of our great country.

The pace was often quite grueling, and the schedule took us on a serpentine path that carried us from hot to cold weather and back again often enough to make the threat of catching cold a very serious one. From San Antonio we went through the Southwest, then hit the Deep South, then to the East and New England before turning toward the Midwest and on to the West Coast. We were in big towns like Philadelphia, Cleveland and New York and small ones like Little America (Wyoming), Ishpen (Michigan) and Connersville (Indiana). We had broiling sun in the South, rain in Boston and snow in Albany.

We had little time for relaxation, and Karol, who is quite gregarious and fun-loving, sometimes felt the strain of loneliness and the discouraging unglamorousness of living out of a suitcase. There were few parties, and the pace of our trip frequently ruled out even movies, so the tour was by no means a plush carpet for her. But the appreciation of the crowd and the great publicity she received compensated for the negative factors, and all in all she was quite happy throughout our trip. She had ambitions to become an actress, and I believe they were furthered by the exposure—no pun intended—she got on tour.

I, too, found it frequently frustrating and tiresome, but I tried to bear the depressing moments uncomplainingly, forcing myself to dwell on the happier aspects of the experience, on the great opportunity it afforded me. I sometimes think that most of us who aspire to be tops in our fields don't really consider the amount of work required to *stay* tops. Sure, you can get the leading role in a Broadway show after ten years of struggling as an actor or actress. But once you've gotten that role, you've got to perform it again and again, and the better you are the longer your show is going to run—possibly hundreds or even thousands of performances. That can get to be pretty draggy, but you asked for it, and if you ever wish you could lay down the burden, you merely have to remember the days when you had to do everything but stand on your head to get anyone to notice you.

Those celebrities who think that their one or two successes entitle them to a free and permanent meal ticket in life usually end up as little more than statistics in a record book or names dropped at cocktail parties. It's a great feeling to arrive, and I can't blame anybody for wanting to sit down for a while to catch his breath and bask in glory after he's made it to the top.

But a champ has to defend his championship again and again or to seek new championships. Otherwise he must, by the jungle law that governs athletic competition, be superseded by anyone of a throng of combatants clamoring to supplant him. And if you want to get more philosophical about it, it's the same in life. Even if you never get to be a champ, you're still going to achieve some good things as you go along, but you can't sit there puffed up with pride, saying "Look at me" for the rest of your life. You have to go back to work, and often the work is without reward. Sometimes, in fact, it's less than that, and you get nothing but a handful of dust for all your striving. If it's any consolation to the runners-up and losers in life, it happens to the biggest as well.

Sometimes, as I said, Karol and I would play our match before the Globetrotter game, and at other times we'd take the court during the half-time intermission. Frequently we'd have our exhibition sandwiched in with other forms of entertainment, such as Broadway routines, tumbling and even ping pong, and that sort of thing rubbed against the grain because it seemed to classify us as an "act," a vaudeville bit rather than a serious display of athletic prowess. But I didn't let that kind of resentment eat at me. Life is too short.

Whenever I got a chance, I'd warm up on the basketball court with the Globetrotters, and this in itself was great sport for the crowd. The players at first welcomed me onto the court, and we had lots of laughs as they fed me the ball for lay-up shots or let me try set shots from center court. But I'm not sure they were always completely tickled when I dunked the ball into the basket. Oh, I didn't threaten to take their jobs away, but it was just a bit irritating to see a woman performing with almost as much skill as they, the greatest basketball players on earth. I enjoyed seeing them squirm and decided for a while to withhold the information that I had played basketball a good deal when I was younger. In fact, just that January, before a packed house at the Harlem Branch of the Y.M.C.A., I had starred in a benefit basketball game between the all-girl teams of Sara Lou's All-Stars and Dorothea Towles' Long Stemmed American Beauties.

We Long Stemmers were attired in red leotards with pink net trapezes bedecked with hundreds of red and pink roses. The All-Stars had black leotards, white shorties, berets, sunglasses, cigarette holders and toy French poodles. We and the audience laughed ourselves silly during the game, especially when some of the poodles began examining the uprights supporting the baskets with a view to irrigating them. But there were no serious accidents of that sort, and when the dust settled, we Long Stemmers had beaten the All-Stars 34 to 30—with yours truly scoring 29 out of the 34 winning points. So I was not exactly untrained when I took the court to warm up with the Trotters.

I don't think I can add any more praise to the ac-
claim that's already been given to these superb athletes
and performers, but I do want to say that besides their
public image I found them wonderful gentlemen,
courteous, sympathetic and fun-loving. The fact that
they were Negroes made my tour a little easier to bear,
for it was comforting to have people with me with
whom I could completely drop my guard from time to
time. It's sad to say so, but no matter how liberal,
how well-accepted into the white community, no matter how popular or famous, no matter how unpreju-
diced a Negro may be, most of us have to wear some
sort of mask outside our own group, and it's a relief
to be able to put that mask down from time to time
when we're back with our own kind. You may think
that smacks of racism, but any of you who belong to
a minority race or religion, party or class, or who have
even so much as moved into a new neighborhood will
have to confess that you anxiously seek someone in
your own circumstances to talk to. What white traveler,
for instance, has not been delighted to run into a
countryman overseas after a long stretch of time spent
strictly among natives?

It's only human; Negro has nothing to do with it.

In any event, my basketball practice with the Globetrotters was just a fun thing, and when it came to tennis
I grew quite earnest. We were to play one set, with the
laurels going to the first player to win eight games.

Karol and I had always been rugged competitors, and although, as I've stated, no titles were to be won in these exhibitions, we played as if our lives and honor depended on winning. No one ever complained that we slacked on the tennis court. Unfortunately, I overpowered Karol and won the overwhelming majority of our matches, but she took her defeats with characteristic grace, and believe me, she made me work for my triumphs. And when she beat me, she beat me magnificently. Whoever won, though, the crowds loved our matches, and the tour was an unqualified success.

Until this time I had seen more of the world beyond America's shores than I had of America itself. But our tour gave me an opportunity to see my own land, and it was an unexpected fringe benefit to sample the scope and depth of the United States. As a matter of fact, it was one of the greatest privileges ever bestowed on me. You can study the statistics about our country until your head is throbbing with them, but nothing can remotely compare with the sight of town after town, city after city, of valleys and mountains, deserts and farms, and everywhere people of inexhaustible variety. I was staggered by the breadth and splendor of our land. When you cross the eastern border of Texas or Nebraska in your fast new car and yet find yourself, ten or twelve hours later, still traveling within the same state, you get a sense of magnificence that makes the words of our national anthem and our other patriotic hymns burn in your mind. It was nothing less than a blessing to tour through my country, and at times I would catch myself humming

Oh beautiful for spacious skies,
For amber waves of grain,
For purple mountains' majesty
Above the fruited plain,
America, America, God shed His grace on thee
And crown thy good with brotherhood
From sea to shining sea.

5

Disillusionment

THE tour came to an end in April, 1960, and when I entered New York that month, I felt as if I'd been swept across the country on a tidal wave of good fortune and success. And in a sense I *had* been, but what I didn't know was that the wave was going to leave me stranded high on the beach, and the waters were about to recede before me. That old devil of mine, cockiness, had me firmly by the arm and was whispering a lot of sweet talk about the future, and I'm afraid I listened to it more than a little.

Perhaps you, too, at that moment would have felt confident about the future if you'd stood in my position. I was greeted with a number of interesting offers on my return, and in addition, my manager had set in motion a couple of projects which might turn out quite profitably.

Meanwhile, my bank balance had begun to take on some semblance of respectability, and I figured that as long as I had it and didn't know how long I was going to have it, I might as well indulge in the new experience of spending it. I got myself a beautiful apartment and knew, for the very first time, the satisfaction of having a home of my own. After years on the road, accepting the hospitality of others, I was at last in a position to have a place to come back to, a place where I could return the kindnesses to friends visiting New York. Perhaps you'll think it was extravagant of me, but no one who has been as rootless as I for any length of time will be unsympathetic. A place of your own reflects your identity, tells people who you are and what your address is. It means you're somebody.

But of course, I didn't spend money on myself only. On the contrary, I realized a long-cherished dream of establishing an address for my family. Oh, they weren't gypsies or anything like that. They'd lived at 135 West 143 Street in Harlem for years and years. But their address was Harlem, and that word has an identity of its own.

Harlem is by no means all slum; there are actually some fine and charming sections there. But no matter how well you live in Harlem, the mere pronunciation of the word conveys to the world an image of a sunless trap seething with unhappy and frustrated Negroes, a place of shame and violence.

I've given a lot of thought to what it is in the fabric of a community that makes it a ghetto. A ghetto is a kind of prison without walls, in which the custodians exist as much inside the community as they do outside. The prisoners accuse white people of imposing the vile conditions on them, and I'm not saying there is no truth in their accusations. But the true custodians of the Negro ghetto are fear, ignorance and poverty, and they make it a self-perpetuating institution. Even if you suddenly removed the white world entirely from the perimeter of Harlem and other Negro slums, there would probably be hesitation and uncertainty before the inhabitants took their first steps into the surrounding area.

In my opinion, one of the major reasons for such confusion is that the subsistence conditions of most Negro households make it impossible for parents to pass along inheritances of any decent size to their children. There is no sense of permanence or continuity, and when their parents pass away, the children feel they are starting from scratch just as their folks did. So it becomes of primary importance for the parents to earn, and to be given a fair opportunity to earn, a substantial enough living so that by wise handling of their funds they can provide for their children's future. And the most important provision they can make is for their children's education, because in the cruel slum cycle only education can dispel ignorance, and once ignorance is gone, there is no fear. And needless to say, education enables one to earn the kind of money that *can* be saved if marshaled wisely.

Although I was not exactly what you would call a lady knight in shining armor, I was at least in the fortunate position of having acquired the basic armament for the struggle to break down a small part of the wall surrounding Harlem. I had education, thanks to the magnificent kindness of Dr. Eaton and Dr. Johnson, whom I mentioned before. These gentlemen had enabled me to get my high school diploma in Wilmington, North Carolina. Then Dr. William Grey, president of Florida A&M, on the recommendation of Walter Austin, the tennis coach there, had awarded me a scholarship to help me get my degree.

I had the other kind of education, too, a little experience in the world as a result of my extensive traveling. I had seen conditions around the globe and had gotten a sense of balance which many people trapped in a ghetto or even in the parochial atmosphere of a big city do not get. I had acquired a sense of what was possible, so that things didn't look as dark to me as they might to a ghetto dweller who knows only what he sees around him and what he hears secondhand about the world.

So I had the second ingredient, a little courage to

make a move into the world. And I had the third one, some money. I had been getting $800 per appearance on the tour, and since there were one hundred appearances or so, I had grossed about $80,000. It was a stupendous amount of money, but don't think that all of it, or anywhere near all, was mine. Bear in mind that I had to bear all the expenses of the tour: the salary of Karol Fageros alone was $30,000, and there were also the salaries of my manager, his assistant, and my secretary; there was the cost of the car and the equipment; a percentage of the cost of motel and hotel accommodations, and so on. And this is to say nothing of the cost of my personal equipment and clothing, food, and my obligations to Uncle Sam and his kid brother in New York State. So I wasn't anywhere near being in the position of buying a solid gold Cadillac, even if I'd wanted one.

Ideally, I would have loved to perform a miracle in Harlem, dissolving it overnight and replacing it with a clean, prosperous, healthy community where brotherhood could flourish and the misery of poverty and fear be abolished forever. And there my parents would live, among the friends they've known and loved for decades. But that dream was slightly unrealistic; the alternative was to find a better home for my folks.

So I put a down payment on a ten-room home on Long Island for my parents and brothers and sisters and moved them out there, where they reside today. They don't roll in luxury, I assure you, but when they open their front door they can see the green of grass and the blue of sky, and there is no smell of refuse, no prostrating heat, no fear of violence.

And in my system of values that's luxury enough, brother.

I said that I had been working on some other possibilities during that spring, and by May I had lined up what seemed to me an interesting and potentially lucrative year. The first arrangement, which I'll describe at greater length in the next chapter, was with the Ward Baking Company, makers of Tip-Top Bread, to make personal appearances around the country. I was to speak about my experiences and career and advise young people to whatever degree I could speak authoritatively. At the same time, of course, I was to put in some good words for my sponsor.

But I wasn't giving up tennis for lecturing. No, I had plans to put my racket to its most ambitious uses ever.

For one thing, I turned my eye to Cleveland, where the world's professional tennis championship was to take place. I had the world's amateur championship under my belt, but because I wanted to dispel any lingering doubts about my supremacy—doubts in my own as well as in other peoples' minds—I registered for the pro tournament. A cash award was the prize, along with a percentage of box office proceeds, so a victory could prove profitable as well as prestigious. Or so I ardently believed.

For another thing, I was contemplating another basketball-tennis tour. Because the reception to our Globetrotter foray had been so wonderful, Abe Saperstein invited us to extend our domestic contract to an overseas tour. The terms he offered were generous, and I weighed the proposition quite seriously.

But other voices whispered and beckoned.

You see, in spite of the excellent money which the Saperstein interests had paid the Gibson interests for accompanying the Globetrotters, the lion's share of revenue from the tour went to the Globetrotter corporation. So we got to thinking that if we organized our own basketball teams and toured with them instead, we wouldn't have to sacrifice all that profit to someone else's franchise.

We calculated the proceeds we would have gotten if the basketball-tennis tour had been strictly an Althea Gibson enterprise, and the figures made us just a little giddy with greed. But I'm sad to say that we left out of these calculations an intangible but critical factor, namely the prodigious reputation of the Globetrotters themselves. But we decided that this would not weigh as heavily as all that and, adhering to the beautiful

71

figures on paper, we ruled that consideration negligible. With great regret, then, we told Abe Saperstein that we would have to reject his offer and pass up the opportunity to go abroad with his team. Instead, we formed a team of our own, engaged some outstanding basketball players and coaches, and began lining up appearances across the United States for a fall tour.

Between May 9 and June 17, while these other plans were being set in motion, I contributed my free services to a tennis clinic in New York City. On the courts of Central Park a number of pros, including Bill Talbert, Bobby Riggs, Sarah Palfrey Cooke and I took youngsters in hand and worked with them on the rudiments and refinements of their game. It was one of the most pleasant little tasks I've ever had to perform. The kids were eager and usually quite solemn in the way they sought and took instruction, and I felt as if I were a farmer supervising the growth of tender buds into strong shoots. Just the mere chance to get some fresh air in the park did something for these kids, and I've always believed that if cities didn't have parks, life in them would be an unmitigated horror. It's as if parks are safety valves through which city dwellers, their souls driven in upon themselves by the brutality of concrete and the bitterness of wintertime, can unleash all that pent-up energy and hostility and harness them to constructive ends.

72

I had a more selfish reason, too, for volunteering for the tennis-instruction program. I wanted to get some experience toward the day when I would be starting my own tennis academy. And in that short month I learned a surprising lot about the psychology of youth and the dynamics of sports education. I learned a few things about myself, too, which can be summed up in the word *patience*. Whenever I felt myself growing frustrated with a child for not grasping my lesson perfectly, I looked back at my own life and saw clearly how long it had taken me to achieve any degree of steadiness and "teachability." I sometimes think I'm still far from having achieved it.

Of course, you can't create a tennis star in a day or even in a month, which was all the time I had. So it was sad for me to leave just when some of my pupils were beginning to show progress. I began to worry that everything I had taught them would be forgotten and abandoned as soon as I was gone.

But that, I see now, isn't the point. The point, rather, is that at the very least I had helped give them a month of fun and a little of the glamor that goes with being able to say you took instruction from a world's champion. But my services might have done even more than that. Perhaps by straightening out a child's swing or serve or strategy, I had given him just the push he needed to enable him to develop his game on his own.

Perhaps by encouraging a few of them, I had helped them to determine on a life of tennis playing or just on a pastime which would keep them out of trouble and fit in later years. I know that even the tiniest morsels of encouragement I received as a young girl boosted my spirits far out of proportion to the words spoken or the pat on the fanny that says, "Nice going, kid." It's not for us to know how far our influence will carry. I firmly believe that you've got to do your best and not worry about the consequences, for the ripples from the pebble you drop in a lake will lap on shores you never dreamed of.

That fall, I went to Cleveland and entered the world's professional championship matches, sponsored by Pepsi-Cola, and I won the female title without difficulty, beating Pauline Betz Addie in three sets. Needless to say, I was quite proud, for now there could be no disputing that I was unbeatable by any woman playing, amateur or professional. But somehow the pride was without depth. It was as if an apparently sumptuous dinner had left me hungry.

When I looked at the check I got for my accomplishment, my jaw dropped: it hardly paid my expenses for the trip to Cleveland. Just as serious, however, was the fact that my title led me nowhere. In the past, title winners had been avalanched with offers to appear in some public exhibition or go on some tour or teach at some club. But the only avalanche that hit me was one of silence, and that much silence can suffocate you.

It was well known that professional tennis was no longer the compelling event it had once been. After the enormous following it had had in the 1930's and 1940's, it had begun to drop away as other spectator sports, like football and basketball, took its place. Accordingly, the purses had depreciated, too. Bill Tilden's tour early in the 1930's had grossed $238,000. The 1948 Pancho Gonzales-Jack Kramer tour grossed $250,000, and in 1949 Kramer had teamed up with Bobby Riggs to launch an international tour that gained them $248,000 in the United States and $135,000 overseas. And even as late as 1952 a tour consisting of Kramer, Frank Sedgman, Kenneth McGregor and Pancho Segura took in a gross of $500,000 for the first fifty matches. But as the immortals dropped away, one by one, from active participation, the sport failed to attract brilliant newcomers, and of course that depressed attendance until the sport spiraled downward. Tennis did not die by any means, and it still draws large and enthusiastic crowds, but I believe that its golden age may be passing.

There were some people, for instance, who denied that the 1960 matches in Cleveland really constituted a world's championship. But even if not everyone denied it, many did ask "So what?" when they read the results. Yes, it was undeniable that something vital was going out of pro tennis. I only have to point out that 1960, the year in which I played, was the last in which the women's division of the professional tennis championship held matches. There has been recent talk of reviving it, though, I'm glad to say, and I'd like nothing more than to see it restored to its former glorious position.

The taste of disappointment was distinctly bitter to me. I was willing to grant that pro tennis just wasn't what it once had been and that public interest in the sport had declined. But when I looked around me, I saw that white tennis players, some of whom I had thrashed on the court, *were* picking up offers and invitations. Suddenly it dawned on me that my triumphs had not destroyed the racial barriers once and for all, as I had—perhaps naïvely—hoped. Or if I did destroy them, they had been erected behind me again.

In a way this kind of prejudice is even more disheartening than the kind that militates against an unknown Negro player, as I had been early in the 1950's. The world discriminates against all unknowns and rookies, whatever their color. So a Negro with no particular reputation or title to his credit could conceivably mistake snobbery for color prejudice. But once a Negro has established himself and the snubs still come, does he really have any alternative but to believe he is being discriminated against by virtue—or I should say, by vice—of his skin? I have always tried to give the benefit of the doubt to universal emotions like snobbery and suspiciousness when I've felt hostility against me; these are understandable and, though unpleasant, at least forgivable most of the time. But when it's apparent that the hostility is directed at my color, I boil over with indignation.

Something happened to me after I won that championship. It was something which, if you'd predicted it a year or two before, I would have suggested you treat yourself to a long rest cure at a funny farm.

I began to lose interest in tennis.

It was not the "No more worlds to conquer" syndrome, as far as I'm able to analyze it honestly. It's true that when you've established your title unequivocally, there's a momentary feeling of boredom. But it *is* momentary, and if you're made of championship stuff, you snap back with a lusty desire to defend your crown against all comers—that is, if the world doesn't deprive you of your desire to do so. But the world had begun to fill me with a sense of futility, almost disgust. Of what value was a room full of trophies and a scrapbook full of praise when you have on your tongue the bitter taste of man's inhumanity toward you? The song on my lips might have been "Ol' Man River":

77

You and me, we sweat and strain,
Body all achin' and wracked with pain.
Tote that barge, lift that bale,
You get a little drunk and you land in jail.

In spite of this growing disillusionment, I picked up my racket and met the next challenge with all my might. This was the tour of the United States that our Gibson Enterprises had arranged. We had lined up our two basketball teams and the tennis exhibition and had a strong itinerary which would carry us through the heartland of the country. As winter settled over the nation, the tour thrust westward.

But the frost wasn't merely outside; the reception we got was as cool as a Canadian wind.

The fear that I had expressed—but foolishly *suppressed*—earlier, when we considered starting a tour of our own, had turned out to be justified. A prime reason for the immense turnouts on our tour with the Globetrotters had been the Trotters themselves. They compelled fanatic allegiance, and furthermore, their well-planned, veteran business organization had far more extensive connections than mine.

And so, as I took to the court before half-empty houses, I began—alas, too late—to understand something about business which had never been clear to me until then. You see, the Globetrotters may have

78

pocketed the greater part of the profits on that tour, but they had also assumed the greater share of the risk. If not a single soul had shown up to watch the Globetrotter-Gibson tour, Abe Saperstein would still have been obliged to pay us the money they owed us in the contract. In other words, even if the Trotters lost hundreds of thousands of dollars on that tour, it would not come out of our pocket. Not even a penny. The risk was all theirs, and we were contractually more like paid employees than partners. But because they took such a risk, they were entitled to the bulk of the profits.

Thus, what I had failed to see clearly was that if I stood to make the bulk of the profits on my own tour, I also stood to absorb the entire loss as well. And the way we were heading, the loss looked to be entire indeed. As a matter of fact, after three months we were forced to cancel the balance of the tour. When the ledgers were examined, they disclosed a loss of between $20,000 and $25,000.

I was, in effect, ruined.

But the disaster didn't end there. Financial ruin is a terrible experience to undergo, but if you can manage to keep your friendships alive in the midst of it, you can bear it philosophically. But the ruin of loyalty is something I find almost impossible to bear courageously, and when that began to crumble, I knew that the catastrophe was going to be the most serious set-back of my entire life.

When things go well, men can afford to be expansive and generous, and partners in an enterprise exist in an atmosphere of mutual-goodwill and love. But when there's a downward turn in fortune, it can often bring out the ugly aspects of human nature. I remember reading about a party thrown to celebrate the signing of a movie contract valued at tens of millions of dollars. The producer and director and actors all held their glasses up and grinned broadly when the producer said, "I always cherish moments like these because I'm keenly aware that six months from now, we're going to be suing each other." And six months later, these people filed solemnly into the courtroom.

As soon as the Gibson ship began to sink, the other principals began grabbing whatever they could salvage, even though it was highly debatable that the things they grabbed belonged to them. I don't wish to name names or expose in public the behavior of those who not only abandoned and betrayed me but, in my estimation, bilked me as well. That episode, with all of its heartbreak and horror, is done with. Though the lesson I learned from it is one of the sharpest of my life, I don't want to stir up old quarrels, blame anyone or express recriminations.

But I do think there is a lesson in my experience that

should be hammered home with all my might, because some of you, perhaps most of you, are bound to enter into business enterprises in good faith. If you don't keep your eyes open, you stand to bring on yourself more grief than you ever thought possible.

Every one of us, when he is presented with a business opportunity, is faced with a crucial decision: whether or not to trust the people he's dealing with. It's normal enough to be suspicious of the man on the other side of the bargaining table because he has his self-interest in mind while you have yours, and those two interests are not always in harmony. But we tend to drop our suspiciousness when it comes to the people who claim to be on our team: a partner, a lawyer, a business manager or accountant, for instance. It's hard to imagine that if someone is working toward the same goal you are, he would injure you if that goal weren't achieved. You would think he'd shrug, as you do, and, following the golden rule, say, "Well, we're all to blame equally for this mistake, and we should all now pay equally for it."

But I'm afraid human nature isn't always as generous as that, especially when the bankroll is involved. People you've loved and trusted in fair weather can turn, in adversity, a side of their faces you never knew before, a side that is pretty hideous.

The problem we all have is that we're afraid to be

81

suspicious. If your lawyers say to you, "Don't bother reading this document. Just sign it and trust that I've arranged everything in your best interests," you're naturally afraid of saying to him, "I want to read it anyway." You think that if you raise that question, he'll get insulted and perhaps will refuse to represent you. But how do you know that when a man says he knows what your best interests are, he and you are talking about the same thing? Unfortunately, most of us are a little vain, and we figure that *everyone* knows what our best interests are. But if you turn the proposition around, you realize that you can't always tell what's best for someone else, even if that person is your own flesh and blood.

So the answer is that you have to be cautious even in your dealings with those who are on your team, or claim to be. You have to read and reflect on every document you sign, no matter how highly your advisers praise it. It's a good idea to get more than one opinion, because other points of view shed unexpected hues of light on a matter and show facets of it you never considered before. It's wise, too, to ask yourself what your business associates might do if your venture flops; are they the kind of people who might turn on you? They might not necessarily do so out of malice, but merely out of a desire to protect their interests from calamity. It doesn't matter what their motives are, however, if you end up the victim.

It's really very sad that the world isn't the kind of paradise where faith is always kept and friendships maintained through thick or thin. It's a shame that we have to say, even to those dearest to us, "I don't mean to be distrustful, but I have to ask for your credentials" or "I want to read the contract myself" or "I'd like to know what your credit rating is." You may indeed give offense to people who feel their character is above questioning. You may even lose some friends. But I hardly think you'll lose any real friends by taking the same precautions with them that you would expect them to take with you. We're afraid to be disliked, but the consequences of being too eager to be liked can be far more disastrous than the loss of a friend.

In brief, as they say in the Las Vegas casinos, "Trust everybody but cut the cards."

6

Breadwinner

I MENTIONED a while back that among the enterprises I involved myself in at the outset of 1960 was a contract with the Ward Baking Company. Since this agreement was to be of paramount importance to me in the grim years ahead, I think it would be a good idea to elaborate on it.

Grey Advertising had arranged a meeting with Ward in the first months of 1960. They were, and still are, a very large company, having at that time twenty-three bakeries in twenty-one states. They evidently felt that it would lend glamour and prestige to their name and help them expand the market for their products to have a prominent figure serving as their public relations man—or woman.

Happily they saw fit to bestow that honor on me, and

I therefore signed a one-year contract with them to act as what they called their community relations representative. Quite fortunately, by the way, this contract was between Ward and me personally, rather than between Ward and my corporation, so that when the corporation met with disaster, the contract with Ward was not affected. In any case, it was decided that at the end of the one-year term of the agreement, Ward and I would make up our minds as to whether we wanted to renew it. If we did, we'd extend it another year, and so on, year after year.

Ward paid me an excellent salary: $25,000 for my year's services. I hope you're not thinking of any puns like "That's a lot of dough from a bread company," because columnists exhausted all the corny jokes describing this arrangement. My deal with them was by no means like the deals some celebrities have, whereby they get a fat fee simply for the use of their names to endorse a product. As a matter of fact, I had to work for my Ward's paycheck, and work hard. You couldn't accuse me of . . . loafing (ouch).

What Ward wanted me to do was to travel from city to city, making appearances on radio and television, at civic functions, school assemblies, charity affairs and society luncheons. The itinerary promised to be a taxing one simply because it would run parallel to other contractual commitments I had or was planning—tennis tours, singing engagements and the like. But we tried to arrange it so that when I was in some city for a sports or performing function, I could also sandwich in—no more puns, I promise—a visit in my capacity as Ward's representative.

The appointment was announced early in March, and there was a lovely luncheon thrown in the Basildon Suite of the Waldorf-Astoria hotel in New York to kick off the program. R. Arnold Jackson, president of Ward, said that the qualities of initiative, courage, stamina and the ability to move ahead on your own are as necessary to success in business as in sports. "Miss Gibson," he concluded, "has demonstrated that she has all of these qualities in good measure. As a sports fan and an Althea Gibson fan, it gives me great pleasure to welcome her to Ward."

Speaking before that luncheon, I announced my intention to establish an Althea Gibson Awards program. A board of judges made up of community leaders would annually pass on award candidates submitted by local organizations of recognized standing. "The award categories will provide added incentive for greater achievements by local young people in scholarship and athletics," I said. I looked forward to experience I might gain, making my rounds for Ward, that would guide me when I established my academy.

Thus my services for Ward began, and whenever

there were open dates in my schedule that spring, summer and fall, I would travel to one of the cities where Ward had a bakery and put in an appearance. Sometimes I didn't have to do more than sit on the dais of a fancy dinner or on some panel of notables. At other times I took a more active role as judge at a talent show or sports contest, selected winners or handed out prizes. In Detroit, for example, Radio Station WCHB and Ward mutually sponsored a city-wide talent contest for children up to twelve years of age. The contest was to be held during the station's fourth annual picnic, and prizes valued at over $500 were to be awarded. I was on the panel of judges, along with executives of Tip-Top Bread, members of the press, and a Detroit television celebrity with the delightful name of Poop Deck Paul. Some 6,000 to 9,000 children and adults turned out, making the event an overwhelming success. It was important enough to cause the Detroit *Courier* to devote an editorial to it, praising the sponsor, the participants, and even the audience whose conduct was orderly when it might, as often happens at such large public affairs, have gotten out of hand.

For the most part, my job as Ward's goodwill ambassador was to speak. My engagements were divided between radio or television interview programs and school assemblies. The interviews were often geared to the women's audiences, and so I'd slant my conversation to subjects that might appeal to ladies. Some of the programs were aired on Negro stations, and I would then describe problems and experiences I'd had with particular reference to being a Negro.

As for the school assemblies, I would address them on my childhood and teen-age days, my career, and the private and public struggles I'd fought. I hoped to inspire my audiences with the courage to overcome their fears, their natural handicaps and the artificial barriers that militate against them. I spoke of humility in victory and fortitude in defeat. Often, at the end of my talk, I would call for questions. Usually the questions were intelligent, but sometimes the children sought to find out something I had told them just ten minutes before. It made you wonder if you'd been wasting your breath.

All in all, though, it was a pleasure to speak before youngsters. They were for the most part attentive and considerate, and I thanked my stars there weren't too many in the audiences who were as sassy as I'd been when I was that age. If there had been, I might have been lucky to escape with my life.

As a finale I would sing a song, and on the majority of occasions I selected my theme song, "So Much to Live For." I was rarely blessed with an accompanist or with one who knew the song or could learn it quickly or sight-read the score. So it behooved me to sing *a capella*—that is, without any accompaniment whatsoever. That's a scary proposition, believe me; you have no instrument to give color to the stark notes you sing or to drown out the nervous quaver in your voice. Yet I handled my singing well, I thought, and was always gratified to receive tumultuous applause and appreciative speeches from the kids and teachers.

The big enemy for me was tedium. I'm not, as you've undoubtedly guessed, so modest that I hate talking about myself. If I didn't think I had something interesting about myself to say, I wouldn't write books, would I? Still, it can wear you down to relate time and again the highlights of your own life, and though I rarely had embarrassing or profoundly thought-provoking questions put to me, I half hoped some little devil in the audience would refresh my enjoyment in having to recount my autobiography.

Of course, I had to plug my sponsor's product, but it wasn't as if they made me do full-blown commercials. Just a few mentions of the Ward Baking Company or Tip-Top Bread were sufficient to get the message across, thank the Lord, and since I really *was* grateful to the company for its generosity, it was never a strain for me to work their name into my conversation naturally and with genuine enthusiasm.

Advertising people sometimes underestimate their

audiences, whom they lump into the category of "markets." But anyone with an ounce of sensitivity, looking into the individual faces that compose an audience, knows that they do not merely constitute a bread-buying market or a car-buying market or any other kind of market. The faces simply belong to people, and people can detect any hint of insincerity in the behavior of a person plugging a product. I could no more have plugged Ward insincerely than I could have saluted a hostile flag.

I don't know if my attitude sold bread or not, but apparently it endeared me to my sponsors because they were to renew my contract four more times, until 1965.

In the first months of 1961 I surveyed my past and my prospects and realized that my own theme song had become a mockery on my lips. So much to live for? What, really, *did* I have to live for?

I had no offers to join a tennis tour.

I had no offers to become a teaching pro at a club.

I had no significant tennis tournaments ahead of me.

I had no singing engagements.

I had no movie engagements.

I owed almost $25,000.

Everything worth living for, it seemed to me then, existed in the past; money, glory, prestige, popularity and publicity, love and friendship, all glowed with the yellowed luster of unpolished trophies.

I awoke one morning and knew the chilling loneliness of one who foresees that he will be forgotten.

Oh, it wasn't as if I had been cast on the refuse heap of society. I still had friends and family, a home, and the raw material of my talents which I could still mold into a potent instrument. And I did, after all, have in my Ward contract a means of making a living and of fighting my way out of debt. And I still had the heartwarming applause of audiences I visited for Ward. But there was an emptiness in life for me now. The applause and the kind words of my friends made me feel like a caged tiger in the zoo. You gasp at how big and great it is—but after all, how much harm can it do anymore?

Well, I hadn't been rendered harmless, at least not permanently, but I felt bereft of purpose and conviction. The praise and accolades I received as I toured and lectured and sang were directed at someone who was once somebody. I was an ex—former amateur champion, former pro champion, former Woman Athlete of the Year, former movie actress, former recording artist.

We're fortunate that our society reveres its ex's and rewards them simply for reiterating their lives and exploits before an admiring public. Many has-beens can finish out their lives on a kind of pension paid them by a world which remembers nostalgically their performance in this film or that championship match.

Others are too proud to let their past accomplishments carry them through life that way. They resent it that no one recognizes them as humans, that people prefer to worship them as luminaries from another age. And they are bitter that no one will even let them turn their abilities to some other form of work. These poor figures are pressured to make some kind of pitiful comeback, and with the exception of a few truly outstanding men and women who do manage to summon up their strength and come out of retirement to prevail once more, most of these characters simply flash across the sky for a moment and then fade forever, leaving a few cinders and the statistical record of their accomplishments.

But neither of these choices held any appeal to me. I was too honest to rest on my past achievements and too bitter to exploit those achievements any longer. I had my contract with Ward and would do my utmost to fulfill it and to speak before audiences without conveying to them any of the disillusionment I felt. But aside from that, I was not about to fall into either of the two traps that await the star who has suffered a setback: the has-been trail or the comeback trail. I would not permit myself the self-pity of the former or the gushy sentimentality of the latter.

Instead I allowed myself only the realistic attitude

that due to a combination of my own mistakes and the ugly ingratitude of the world, I had been handed a humiliating defeat. I would withdraw to familiarize myself with this new sensation; I would reflect on my errors; I would contemplate the fact that the world can be as hellish as it can be heavenly. But I would not abandon faith. I would explore my resources and discover new strengths; I would marshal them together until I had command of myself once more. And when they responded to my will as perfectly as my muscles had once responded when I'd played tennis, I would go forth and challenge again.

7

From Rackets to Clubs

YOU can color the next two years gray for Althea
Gibson. They involved an immense amount of labor
and a singular lack of glamor. I devoted myself almost entirely to my duties for Ward. I traveled exten-
sively, but this time there was none of the thrill of
discovery I had felt when touring with the Globetrotters. I traveled alone, and if I didn't have friends
to put me up in the cities I visited, I would take a
room in some unpretentious hotel. Frequently I chose
to stay in when I had some free time, instead of sight-
seeing or seeking entertainment or the company of
other people. Sometimes I just stared at the ceiling,
and when that form of diversion became too dull, I'd
roll on my side and stare at the walls.

I fulfilled my goodwill job for Tip-Top with as much

goodwill as I could exercise. But I was weary with myself and grew discouraged with the routine. Not only did I have to repeat myself time and time again, but now the repetition didn't even have the fresh delivery of one who likes oneself, enjoys oneself, is interested in oneself. I couldn't believe in myself enough to talk about Althea Gibson with conviction. And when I sang my song, it was with an almost ironic delivery. You can't sing about how much you have to live for when that constitutes a nondescript hotel room in a strange city. But I wasn't going to let my sponsor or my audiences down, especially the young children. What kind of example would I be setting if I showed them I couldn't be as strong in adversity as I'd been in victory?

Although I had during that time numerous opportunities to play tennis, I just couldn't bring myself to take advantage of them. As a matter of fact, I was beginning to develop an actual indifference to tennis. It was as if the racket were coming to symbolize the futility of ambition and the meaninglessness of success. At last, in an interview with a sports reporter during this period, all of the rancor in my heart boiled over, and I told him, "I don't care if I ever pick up a tennis racket again."

I imagine that was the lowest moment of my career. But two highlights shine through the murk of the early 1960's. The first is that little by little I was paying off my debts. It was a point of honor with me that I meet these obligations. From my Ward salary for the next five years, I set aside a certain amount regularly toward the satisfaction of my creditors. In the absence of any other really tangible goal, the meeting of my debt became the end I lived for. I doubt if any record book carries statistics on debts paid off, but if it did, you would find in it as many tales of heroism and endurance as there are in the annals of sports. I looked at this challenge as one as crucial as any I'd ever faced in my athletic career.

Although I wouldn't wish debts on anybody, they're an interesting experience to live through. I'm reminded of a line from Tennessee Williams' play *Cat on a Hot Tin Roof,* when Big Daddy, suffering from a heart ailment, declines his medicine, saying, "As long as I'm in pain, I know I'm alive." It was the same for being in debt. Earlier in my life, it had been a source of pride for me to be able to say, "I've earned twenty-five thousand dollars." Now, with whatever pride I had left, I pointed to my debt and boasted, "How many people can claim they owe twenty-five thousand dollars?" It isn't easy to run up such a huge bill!

And so my debt became my identity for a while, and until the day when I could say that I was once again earning large sums, I would comfort myself with the knowledge that I owed more money than most people earn in a year—and that I was nevertheless repaying it. It may sound a little eccentric, but when your alternative is despair, you frequently have to settle for a lot of eccentric thoughts to console yourself with.

More important by far, though, was the first faltering step I took on the golf course.

I had played golf before, of course, and I even mentioned it as a future possibility in the statement I released in 1958 announcing my retirement from amateur tennis. But aside from a few rounds in the succeeding years played for relaxation, I hadn't gone out on the links at all. When I did, I certainly didn't think of golf earnestly as a new career from which I could make a living and even win money and honors.

But after a while on the lecture trail for Ward, something began to happen to me. I got bored and angry with myself for my inactivity and withdrawal from life. I began to get restless for the keen pleasure of competition. My muscles began twitching with a desire to engage in taxing activity. And my heart began to long for a goal more fulfilling than the repayment of a debt.

I hearkened back to the encouragement I'd gotten from golf pros and sports commentators. Gus Salerno, the Hampshire pro from Westchester, has said of my potential in 1959: "Althea has everything. The swing, the hands, the touch, the temperament. I hit real good, .

but she was up with me on drives. I guarantee she can outdrive 50 percent of the pros. She's smart, she's cool, she listens and likes to learn. Of course, Althea needs polishing. She hasn't played much, but give her a year of work and she could be the greatest. Right now she's driving about two hundred fifty yards without really letting out. She lacks the knowledge and experience to release all her power at this point."

Jerry Volpe, the owner-pro at Englewood, had said of me, "Fabulous. That girl hits just like a man. She has a big, easy swing and wonderful hands. With practice, I don't see how she can miss. She'd give pro women's golf a terrific jolt. Upward, I mean."

Columnist Gene Roswell had said, "Althea has the muscle and coordination for basketball and baseball, the speed and finesse for tennis, the touch and delicacy of control for pool and ping-pong, and the cold aplomb for golf. Put these all together and you have the makings of the greatest all-around woman athlete since the late Babe Didrikson Zaharias. Maybe greater. To establish it, Althea would have to turn to competitive golf as the Babe did in capturing every major distaff title for women, from the U.S. and British Amateur championship to the U.S. Open, then on to professional eminence."

Yes, a lot of people thought I might go far in golf, and as I began to stretch my limbs and awaken after a

kind of hibernation, I dared to think so, too. But that
road was littered with obstacles and menaces of every
kind, and in my frame of mind the outlook was so discouraging that I hesitated to commit myself to the
challenge with my usual enthusiasm.

For one thing, not even counting the external hazards, there was the problem of my own ability. In
spite of the inspiring words I've just quoted, I had a
lot of deficiencies working against me. Tennis and golf
are in many ways at opposite ends of the spectrum
from each other. Tennis requires enormous speed and
power; golf is a deliberate and casual sport; though
power helps in golf, it isn't an absolute necessity and
can even be a hindrance. Tennis provides a visible
opponent on whom, to a great degree, you depend for
the quality and pace of your game; golf, though you
do play against opponents, technically speaking, is es-
sentially a solitary challenge. It's you against the ball,
you against distance, you against nature. Above all, it's
you against yourself, struggling with your muscles, timing and coordination for precise control of the swing.
There's nobody to blame if you lose. It's all you.

The physical and mental shift from one kind of game
to another, especially if you're thinking in championship terms, is extremely difficult to make. My age, too,
might be a handicap. I was approaching thirty-three,
and while that isn't intended to mean I was ready for

a home for the aged, thirty-three is considered "getting along" in most sports. The reflexes begin to slow down after thirty, and I had the added problem of adjusting my reflexes from tennis conditions to those of golf. I was thus faced with an unusual adjustment.

Even if there were no other handicaps to overcome, these would be quite enough to grapple with.

But there were others. One of them was money. I needed equipment, and I needed someplace to play. I needed professional instruction as well. I couldn't afford a private club, and even public links demanded fees. I didn't have to be a millionaire to enter the sport, but I would need a decent amount of backing.

I turned my thoughts to Ward.

I didn't know how my sponsors would feel if their community relations representative, appointed for her prowess as a tennis player, threw over tennis for the game of golf. The contract with them was renewable on a year-to-year basis, and if it was canceled at the end of the first year I'd have absolutely no source of income. But if I could hold onto the Ward contract and persuade the directors to support me in this new venture, at least I'd have some money to work with. I could divert some of it toward golf expenses and try to persuade my creditors to accept a slowdown in the repayment of my debts. I would have to demonstrate to these creditors that this arrangement represented a

101

kind of investment for them: if I played golf well enough I'd turn pro, and my winnings would enable me to pay my debt to them in the last analysis.

I had no idea whether the people to whom I owed money would look at the situation with the same eyes that I did; creditors and debtors rarely, it's a notorious truth, see life in the same terms. If they thought my desire to play golf frivolous, they could create a good deal of hardship for me and in fact ruin my plans. An uncompromising attitude on their part would have the effect of taking away from me the very tools by which I hoped to make a living.

And of course I was aware of the biggest roadblock of all: the color of my skin. Even if I'd had enough money to belong to a private club, where I would have the best facilities for developing my game, it was highly questionable that many clubs would extend me membership. Negro golfers in the early part of this decade were more of a rarity than they are now. It was not realistic to believe that one—and a woman, at that— would be welcome in any private club.

All right then, I'd practice on public courses, that's all. But *was* it all? Even if I did develop my game into championship quality, I would be competing on private courses. Would I be permitted to play on all of them? Some of my more pessimistic advisers feared that I would not. Although most states have laws protecting individuals against such discrimination, those laws can be circumvented through political or financial pressures, thus depriving a Negro or member of some other minority group of his rights. In this way, then, my means of making a living would be blocked. I still wouldn't be able to repay my debts, to say nothing of getting a decent crack at becoming a championship golfer.

The warnings and derision flew around my head like a flock of mocking crows, but the more I thought about it, the more determined I became not to let all those objections stand in my way. In fact, there is a perverse wrinkle in my nature that relishes obstacles, looks forward to them and even seeks them out for the pleasure of wrestling with them and throwing them out of my path.

So I examined the problems and discussed with myself what equipment and strategies I might employ for overcoming them.

I was certain I had natural ability as a golfer and, as I had promised myself a long time before, I wasn't going to let any natural ability of mine go unexploited as long as there was a chance that I could achieve something out of the ordinary with it. As for my age, golf luckily is the kind of sport that accommodates the muscles and reflexes of athletes of all ages. It is by no means a young people's sport in the way, for instance, that championship swimming is. As a matter of fact, we don't develop many of the abilities and attitudes necessary for competence in the game of golf until we're in our thirties and forties. Patience, concentration, self-control, discipline, judgment, relaxation, timing are all virtues which mature with age. Read, for instance, what Tom Scott and Geoffrey Cousins say on the subject:

The middle-aged golfer is like a gourmet appreciating the flower, the bouquet and the flavor of a cherished claret. The young golfer is like a coarse feeder washing down a steak with a pint of bitter. Each thinks he has the best of what the world can offer. But only the middle-aged golfer can compare steadily the value of untutored strength with the value of experience.

That quotation is from their book *Golf Begins at 45,* and if what they say is true, I was still a mere baby at thirty-three, with all my most important lessons and triumphs ahead of me. Many people thought it remarkable that I was taking up a new sport in my thirties. How often I heard that old chestnut about old dogs and new tricks! But I would tell them it's never too late to start any enterprise in which you believe you can be productive, or which you believe will satisfy your needs.

So I ruled out any objections on the grounds of

ability or advancing years. As for the money problem, I could only try. I would speak to Ward and ask them to back me by renewing my contract and endorsing this new course I was taking with my life. And I would ask my creditors for patience, understanding— and time.

The problem of my race might be a serious one, but I was not without the resources to cope with it. I'd had abundant experience with discrimination and was familiar with ways of handling it. Through exercise of patience, firmness and self-confidence and with the help of sympathetic friends, public institutions and laws, I could put up a good fight against any barriers erected against me. My name still carried considerable weight, and I reckoned on that kind of publicity to support me. In addition, I saw that once I received my player's card from the Ladies' Professional Golf Association, I would be entitled to the same privileges as they. That would mean I would have a kind of family to assist me in getting a fair shake at those golf clubs that might otherwise balk at letting me play.

And so the primary consideration was for me to become a good golfer, good enough to compete, good enough to challenge, good enough to win. And if I was thus good enough to beat the top women pros and thus satisfy the membership requirements of the L.P.G.A., I'd have conquered the biggest dragon guarding the tower of success: myself.

8

Hope Revisited

I WAS enormously heartened by the support I got from my friends and family and from Ward, when I announced my determination to take up golfing in a serious way. People have an instinct for knowing whether you're really serious or not when you make a decision. If you are, they flock to you with encouragement, but if you're not, they nod and mutter grudging approval and nothing more. And I knew from the way they rallied to me that I must have been radiating sincere resolution.

Ward indicated it would not only renew my contract but would do its best to permit me time off to practice and play. I must say I took advantage of this generous attitude. With my usual all-or-nothing method of operation, I began playing every minute I could spare.

I would show up on the public courses at eight in the morning and play until it was too dark to see the flags.

I got some funny looks, I can tell you, as I signed in on the course waiting lists and took my place on the practice tee or putting green among the white males. But stares were nothing new to me, and they frequently turned to wide-eyed gazes of appreciation, respect and even envy when I stepped up to the tee and walloped a drive over two hundred and fifty yards down the fairway.

As I began to feel the restoration of purpose, my spirits rose and I became alive again. Reporters, noticing that I was putting in a lot of time on the links, began asking what it signified, as if they didn't know. I let out cautious remarks about the possibility of a new career, but I held back from making earth-rending declarations. Any budding talent I had might be nipped by premature announcements to the effect that Althea Gibson was launching a new career and casting her eye on the women's golfing crown, etc. Well, you know how reporters talk.

For once in my life, I needed no publicity. I needed peace and calm and an unhindered opportunity to work on my game.

Though the public links were crowded, and during hours of peak course traffic I was forced to team up with other players, there was still a sense of solitude about the game for me, of being a self-contained entity accountable to no one but myself. There was no feeling of "engaging" an opponent, of pitting my might and skill and intelligence against another human. If anything, I felt great camaradarie with the players at my side, moaning when one missed a putt or messed up a drive, cheering when one drove a long ball or placed an approach near the pin. In tennis, of course, you can't afford to be too generous to your opponent, because after all, her every gain is your loss and vice versa. But in golf, though I suppose in the last analysis your opponent's good playing will take bread out of your mouth, you really can't get up the spleen to wish unkind thoughts on the player at your side. That's why golf is truly a game of friendship and why it has a reputation for providing an atmosphere in which business, political and professional dealings can be carried out amicably and successfully. The rivalry is always friendly, and you almost never hear of enmities, feuds or grudges on or off the golf circuits.

I say I had a sense of solitude, but that doesn't necessarily imply loneliness. I had begun to learn to live with the idea of being alone, and the bitter experience of the past two years had even taught me to like it and find virtue in it. Besides, now that I had a little direction again, I didn't feel the stark loneliness of the days when there was nothing bigger than me, nothing beyond my reach, to strive toward. Having a purpose is like having another person by your side, frowning at you when you err and applauding you when you progress. A soul gets to talking to herself a lot that way, I guess, but except for being astonished at the variety of oaths my other self used when she was bawling me out, I got used to it.

In fact, strongly in contrast to the loneliness of being alone were moments of almost excruciatingly poignant happiness. If you've ever been out on a golf course alone, at dusk of a perfect summer day, and you've stopped to listen to the sound of the world spinning through the universe, you know what I mean. I had to caddy for myself then, and so I might pause on the fairway to remove the heavy bag from my shoulder and lean on it for a minute or two. The relief from its weight evoked a floating sensation, and the release from the rhythmic jangle of the clubs made the stillness around me as sharp and clear as the report of a pistol.

If the course were deep in the country, the silence could be absolute except for the twitter of birds fussing with their nests before settling in for the evening. But if the course were located in the suburbs of a city, I could hear a kind of muffled roar in the air, like the sound of a train moving way off in the distance.

I would look before me and behind me, and there

would be no one. I could imagine what it might be like to be the only person on earth. To a girl raised in the city, the feeling was doubly stirring because there had scarcely been a moment in my life when humans weren't within ten paces of me. But now there wasn't a soul in sight, and the only moving things might be the tops of the trees as the twilight breezes rustled through them.

I was never afraid at these moments. On the contrary, I would be filled with fearlessness as I contemplated the presence of a spiritual Being very grand and very gentle who could provide for us, on a few privileged occasions in our lives, a setting as moving as this by which we could glimpse His scheme. In moments such as these I was thankful for the blessings bestowed on me, and any bitterness I felt over the misfortunes in my life fled.

It was funny in a way. Here I hadn't begun to approach the summit of the golfing world, but I'd already stood at the threshold of heaven.

Well, to plunge from the sublime to the mundane, my efforts on public courses were costing me a lot of money. Perhaps the good Lord, watching over me as I meditated on His divine presence on the golf course, listened to my prayers, but in any event I soon got a break which was to be of the utmost importance to me.

Jerry Volpe, whom I mentioned earlier as owner-pro

of the Englewood Club, decided I had a lot of promise and invited me to use the facilities of his club. In fact he made me an honorary member, an eminently gracious act, considering that I was the only Negro, man or woman, on the club's membership roster at that time. In addition, he gave me some tips on my game, and his support at that crucial stage in this tender new life of mine made a major difference for me. For the first time, I was freed from many cares and distractions and could concentrate on my game without that voice of guilt rebuking me for spending money on what might turn out to be a futile endeavor. And for the first time, as I steadied on and played some respectable rounds of golf, I glimpsed a championship form in myself that stilled that other voice and filled me with a growing hope that maybe, just maybe . . .

The years 1961 and 1962, then, were Ward tours and golf, golf and Ward tours, and hard, hard work. Was there anything or anyone else in my life to mitigate this dull pattern? As a matter of fact, there was.

Over a decade earlier—in 1951, to be exact—I had gone to live in New Jersey with the Darben family. Though it was intended that they would put me up for a week to enable me to enter a tennis tournament in that area, I had, like the man who came to dinner, extended my stay somewhat: seven or eight years. The family had taken me in, and one of the six children, Rosemary, had become my closest friend.

112

Another of those children was William. Will had taken a shine to me, and though nothing romantic developed during that time, we saw a lot of each other. He would accompany me to many social functions and the like, and it was therefore rumored that he and I were engaged. But that simply wasn't true.

What is true is that he'd proposed to me in 1953, but out of consideration of my career I decided then that marriage wasn't for me. I turned down the proposal, but fortunately none of the bitter consequences followed that often occur when a bid for a girl's hand is denied. Far from it; Will and I became fast friends and remained so over the years. Thereafter, during good times and bad, we were never out of touch, and the little things he did for me along the way are too numerous to recount.

Although I didn't realize it fully for a long time, I was coming to depend on him. He was like a part of me, but not so much a limb you consciously use; he was more like a vital organ whose existence keeps you alive but which you usually take for granted. He was always in the back of my thoughts and not infrequently in the front of them.

Will had qualities I respected and admired. These had never been so evident, for instance, as when his mother became gravely ill. He had always been devoted to his mother, brothers and sisters, but he now

113

rose to the crisis. His sister had to leave her job to take care of Mrs. Darben, and that doubled the load on Will's shoulders now that Rosemary wasn't bringing home an income. Nevertheless, in his capacity as administrative assistant at the Bendix Company he worked himself almost ill to bring in extra money to support the household and pay for his mother's medical expenses. That discipline bespoke a steady family man who could be relied on to stand by you under the most trying circumstances. I've seen men run away from their responsibilities under similar conditions.

As I say, I was so involved with myself in the fifties that I had to forbid thoughts of a serious romantic nature. A husband during that period, as I look back at it now, might have been a hindrance on my various tours. He would have been placed in the position of my escort, and that would have damaged his pride. We'd no doubt have gotten on each other's nerves. On the other hand, it wouldn't have been fair to ask a husband to stay home while his wife gallivanted all over creation. Even if he weren't the suspicious or possessive type, what kind of life would it have been for him to have a wife away from home most of the year? I see now that these were the typical doubts of a single girl; as a happily married woman, I would look back at them and laugh. But at that time they were most grave.

No, I wasn't ready for marriage then, and none of the men I'd met seemed ready for it, either. Though Will was devoted to me and was certainly the man I would choose if I were choosing at all, I had to reject him—because I was rejecting the whole concept of marriage.

I've described Will as a kind of vital organ which, though necessary for me to function properly, I was not always aware of. But sometimes when your life undergoes a change, you come to appreciate how valuable that organ really is. Let me go into that a little more precisely.

One of the liabilities of being a celebrity is that you're never certain whether someone loves you for yourself or rather for the vicarious excitement of being involved with an important personage. Thus even if I'd wanted to get married during the period when I was in the public eye, I'd have always wondered if my husband had proposed to Althea Gibson the champion or Althea Gibson the woman.

Of course, one good test of a man's sincerity is to become a failure. Though I didn't fail deliberately, I assure you, and certainly am not foolish enough to throw away fame and fortune just for the sake of seeing which of my friends would stand by and which abandon me, the fact that I did have a run of bad luck helped me to see clearly who among my past acquaintances was most loyal to me.

Will Darben had known me long before I had made anything of myself as a tennis player, and he loved me then. He had known me while I was a star, and he loved me then, too. And now I was down on my luck, and still he insisted on loving me. I had no doubt that whatever twist my fate should take in the future, the crazy darling would go on loving me. And so during 1960, 1961 and 1962, Will and I moved closer to one another and reopened the discussion of marriage.

But Althea Gibson is a headstrong gal, I'm afraid, and she likes to take her own sweet time about making up her mind. And if it takes her twelve or fourteen years to do it, you've got to appreciate that she doesn't like to be pushed into any impetuous decisions. So when Will asked me again to marry him, I very coyly, very femininely said no. From the "You just love me because I'm a star" argument, I moved to the opposite pole with the "You just feel sorry for me, I've got to prove I'm worthy" argument.

If anyone had suggested I was just plain scared of marriage, I might have wrapped a pitching wedge around his neck, but when I think about it, I wonder if maybe there wasn't a little truth to that explanation. There was, after all, never a time in my life when I didn't have an excuse for staying single: I was too young, I was too old, I was too successful, I wasn't successful enough, I needed more romance, I needed more steadiness.

116

It began to dawn on me that the only way to find out what marriage was like would be to try it. Nevertheless, during the time we're talking about, I held Will's proposal in abeyance and flung myself into another passionate love affair instead: with a golf ball.

9

A Rookie Again

AS 1962 passed into 1963 the embers of hope, which I'd been fanning incessantly with wooden and steel clubheads, began to kindle into flame. Until then I had kept myself warm only with a vague sense of purpose. But now I had a sense of accomplishment, too. Belief in yourself can carry you far, but until you've proved yourself with results you can't know true satisfaction. Self-confidence is an illusion we create to inspire ourselves, but it must eventually fade if it isn't borne out by achievement.

Of course, if you analyze my achievements in 1961 and 1962, you might not find anything tangible to inspire a belief that I had a future in golf. I won no tournaments, set no records, earned no prize money. No, the achievement was a quiet one, a secret between me and myself.

You see, every professional golfer swings in what he calls a "groove." It's a pattern of arm, wrist, hip and leg motions that constitute a golf swing uniquely his own. A groove comes only after constant practice and play, when the golfer has swung so many times in the same way that he can no longer swing in any other. In brief, it's a habit, and to acquire it demands as much discipline as any other habit, if not more.

I worked intensively, trying to find my groove. A groove doesn't necessarily mean a natural swing, though, because what feels natural is not always correct, and many correct techniques don't feel natural at first. I did have a good natural swing, though, and luckily didn't have to revolutionize it to improve my swing. But I still had lots of work to do on things like stance, grip and muscle control in order to get the utmost out of my body.

Sometimes I'd reach a discouraging saturation point in my practice when all my instructions pecked at me like a flock of angry birds—head still, elbow stiff, wrist flexible, feet this way, hands that way! I was still thinking of the instructions as separate and individual, trying to keep them all in my head and concentrate on them all equally at the same time. I felt like a watchman trying to guard six different warehouses at once. But eventually, one by one, each distinct action reached a level of competence, and I could forget about it for a while in order to concentrate on another one.

My long game—that is, the use of my driver and other woods—never caused me serious trouble, though I did learn some ways of improving distance and direction. More troublesome, however, were my short game and approach shots. I thought of the irons as a fiendish pack of tormentors requiring tremendous control. My long game was good because I could let myself out without restriction, but the short game required me to hold myself in.

Such self-restraint brought out all my impatience, and I had never had to deal with this unpleasant side of myself as firmly as I did now. My professional advisers told me that because of my tennis background, I tended to hook or bring the club down too fast. Lee Young, a drummer for the late Nat King Cole and a low-handicap golfer, gave me some tips on trap shots, those archdevils that haunt most players mercilessly. He told me to hold the club head flat and hit from the outside in, instead of from close inside my body out, when in the bunker. I also had to take the club away from my body on the backswing. Julius Boros also advised me on trap shots. The tips worked, and I gained some measure of success in thrashing the archdevil. But as I told reporter Gene Roswell, "The next thing I have to learn is how to stay out of traps." His reaction to that naïve statement indicated that when I did learn that secret, I should patent it, bottle it and retire a billionaire.

Finally, I had to improve my putting. There is no way to do that but to work from dawn to dusk on it, getting the measure of the pin, judging the slope of the green, assessing the texture of the turf and even accounting for wind. In due time you get into a groove with your putting, too, but I sometimes think it does you no good at all. No two putts—at least those longer than tap-ins—are the same. Or if they are, then *you're not!* Jack Nicklaus is famous for carrying a little black book describing minutely the conditions of each course he plays and the particular shots he has to make, and he refers to that book and adjusts it each time he returns to the course. But I wonder if he remembers to record the condition of his body and his frame of mind, for his internal layout is just as important as the external one of the fairways, roughs and greens, and very often a psychological dogleg or mental bunker can trap you more ruinously than those on the links. In any event, you must constantly reevaluate *all* conditions as you play a course and compensate for changes with the mathematical precision of a missile-tracking computer.

At last the day came, however, when my self-consciousness disappeared entirely, and I didn't have to

122

give special attention to any particular aspect of my swing. Everything fell into place in the mold I had so assiduously prepared. I had my groove.

Although possession of a player's card is the official mark of a professional golfer, his groove is, in a way, really his most important credential. It's as much a symbol of his identity as his birth certificate. It's the ideal golf round he carries in his heart and body at all times, just like the program of that computer. He may deviate from it, may even depart from it radically for a shot or a game or even for a season, but it's always his point of reference.

Naturally, when I realized I'd found my groove, I was terrifically elated—I felt groovy, you might even say. But at the same time, I knew that I had only reached a plateau, the first one. For it meant only that I had completed my apprenticeship, and attached to that diploma is no guarantee that mastery of basics will get you a job or win you any tournaments. It simply entitled me to try, to utilize what I'd learned toward the purpose of making a career for myself. I was now entitled to employ my skill competitively, but it didn't necessarily follow that I would succeed in competition.

The only way to find that out was to compete.

I played in some amateur tournaments and would have been glad to continue as an amateur for a while, but that course was no more realistic than the one of remaining an amateur in tennis. A little thing called money dictated that I apply what I'd learned toward making a living. And so, not without a little trepidation, early in 1963 I informed the Ladies' Professional Golf Association of my intention of becoming a professional golfer.

The process of becoming a card-carrying pro is not especially complicated, but it is not easy, either. Except for invitational tournaments, any approved player applicant can enter a professional tournament simply by paying a fee, the fee being $50 plus .1 percent— one tenth of one percent—of the total prize money offered. If the prize money totaled $15,000, for instance, the additional fee would be $15, and each entrant would pay a total fee of $50 plus $15, or $65. Amateurs with a low handicap who simply want the practice or thrill of competition can enter and, if they're good enough, progress to the final round and indeed to the winner's circle as if they are pros. But they are barred from winning money, and unless they indicate officially a desire to turn pro, their scores aren't applicable toward the gaining of professional status.

When an amateur notifies the L.P.G.A. of her intention to turn pro, her competitive scores are credited toward the issuance of her player's card. In order to get her card, she must finish among the top 80 percent of the pro entrants in at least three out of four consecutive L.P.G.A. cosponsored tournaments. In other words, if there are forty entrants in each of four consecutive tournaments, the aspiring approved player applicant must place thirty-second or better in three of them to merit her card. Once she gets it, though, it's hers forever, revocable only for unprofessional behavior. The card entitles her to all rights and privileges in the L.P.G.A., and of course it's her ticket of admission to most tournaments, fees being dispensed with from that point on.

The biggest day for me in 1963, and in a sense the most important in years, was my debut at the Kenwood Country Club in Cincinnati. I did not, of course, have my player's card, but this was my first tournament since registering my intention to earn it. I had three purposes: to get competitive experience, to win money, and to earn credit toward my card. It will not come as a surprise to you to learn that this first effort of mine didn't set the course on fire. But it was no less thrilling to me for that, representing as it did the beginning of a new life.

So if I didn't bring in a particularly good score that day, it may have been because my feet never quite touched the ground.

I had wondered how the girls on the tour would regard me, the first Negro woman to compete in professional golf. There was a substantial number of Southern girls in the L.P.G.A., and I had no reason to expect them to put out a red carpet for me. But my fears were unfounded. I was warmly and naturally welcomed into the tour, and every girl was as gracious and considerate as she could be.

Of course, if I *had* been ignored or mistreated, it might have been difficult to assign the motivation to racial prejudice. As I've said, it's the Negro's lot, as it is the lot of any member of a minority group, rarely to know beyond the shadow of a doubt that hostility directed at him is due to racial hatred. A new member of any community, whether that community be a golf tour, a suburban neighborhood, a school or even a church, is usually regarded with suspicion at first. A group that is at ease with itself is bound to handle a foreign element entering it somewhat roughly until it's decided whether that element represents a threat or not. Bear in mind that I was a rookie, and rookies of any color are subject to some abuse, not only because they're strangers but because they are, after all, competing with group members for the glory and profit of being Number One—and there's only one Number One.

And so if there ever was frigidity in the air from time to time, I gave the girl the benefit of the doubt and marked it down to the discomfort and strangeness that invariably arises when humans are making their first contact. I reminded myself that I'm not the most openhearted soul in the world on initial meeting and that I could provoke hostility simply by means of my own defense mechanisms.

Getting back to golf itself, the rest of 1963 was to prove discouraging if you're looking for palpable results. I played in only six or seven tournaments and didn't win a farthing. In fact, my average score was 84, and in a game where money rides only on averages in the 70's, my 84 was ridiculously out of the running. But I hadn't really looked to 1963 as a year of earning, but rather as one of learning. Had I gained anything beyond experience that year, I'd have been pleasantly surprised. I had faith in myself to sustain me in lieu of money, though, and consoled myself with the hope that the next year would show a few marks on the credit side of the ledger.

As I say, faith can carry you a long way, but cold cash is a good second choice.

Since I didn't place high in any tournament in 1963, I didn't come close to winning my player's card. But that was the real goal for 1964, and until the tour began in the spring of that year, I practiced relentlessly. I sought help both from club pros and, once the tour was underway, from the girls themselves.

Although some athletes credit profound improvement to the instruction of one person, I can't really say that any special individual had a hand in making my game over, or indeed that I learned any secrets that radically altered my approach to golf. It was a matter of slow, steady gains from constant practice, plus careful attention to the advice given me. As far as that goes, I rather shamelessly requested aid from anyone I thought would give it to me, and numerous people did give it to me so that little by little, details of my performance were improved. But I can still acknowledge some of the golfers who took special pains to help me. Johnny Johnston, for example: an honorary member of Jerry Volpe's Englewood Club, Johnny was the first person to invite me to play at a private club after I began thinking earnestly about golf. And of course, Jerry Volpe himself. Eoline Thornton was instrumental in stimulating me to take up the game seriously. And I was aided immeasurably by Gus Salerno, Mickey Wright, Kathy Whitworth, Marlene Bauer Hagge, Walter Reabley, Jimmy Devoe, Charley Brown, and Gloria Armstrong. Special thanks go to Alice Hovey, Marlene Hagge's sister, who went out of her way on one occasion to give me a lesson in humanity as well as golf. And last but not least, I thank Teddy Rhodes.

10

Just Let Me Play

I ANXIOUSLY looked forward to 1964, regarding it not so much as a year as a battlefield. In the foreground was a pillbox guarding the passage to all enemy terrain. That pillbox held my player's card, and until I'd stormed and subdued it, my chances of securing the objectives beyond it were slim. In the distance those objectives shimmered seductively. Some were as small as tap-in putts, others as grand as trophies; some were as mundane as a new leather golf bag, others as noble as brotherhood. I was eager to lay siege to all of them, but first things first.

Let me give you some idea of the way the ladies' tour is set up. There are between fifteen and twenty-five official tournaments on the spring and summer schedule of the Ladies P.G.A. and perhaps another ten on the fall circuit. When I say "official," I mean those for which players are given credit in L.P.G.A. records—scores, earnings, player standings and the like.

The most important of these are the U.S. Golf Association Women's Open and the L.P.G.A. Championship, held at Pleasant Valley Country Club in Sutton, Massachusetts. The prize money for these two contests is $25,000 and $20,000 respectively. The player or players who walk away from these contests carrying a cup are generally regarded to be the tops, and the record books usually award the overall championship to the girl who wins the U.S.G.A. Women's Open. This contest has been dominated in the last nine years by Mickey Wright, who has won it no fewer than four times since 1958. Some of the other important matches on the official tour are the Lady Carling Open, the Dallas Ciritor Open, and the Supertest Canadian Open.

There are other tournaments during the season which give a player the opportunity to make some money. These are the pro-amateur contests, usually taking one day to play instead of three or four, as in the big tournaments. The prize money is relatively modest—$1,500 or $2,000—and since these are "best ball" contests, where only one partner's score—the best score of the four partners—is counted on each hole, the scores are not counted in the official L.P.G.A. record books. Nevertheless, these tournaments are

130

usually great fun, for they pair pros with local country-club amateurs and/or members of the organization cosponsoring the tournament with the L.P.G.A., and the competition is zestful.

In addition, the girls participate in some nonofficial tournaments which frequently pay big cash prizes. The Yankee Ladies' Team Championship, for instance, pays in the range of $20,000, so if prizewinners in these tournaments don't get their names listed in official L.P.G.A. statistics, they can console themselves with rather impressive checks. There are open dates between all these tournaments when players may, if the L.P.G.A. approves, participate in unofficial tournaments elsewhere.

You can see, then, that a professional golfer can keep herself pretty busy. Some gals, for whom golf is an all-absorbing career, are almost always engaged in one tournament or another, or earn a living in the winter by teaching golf after earning one in the summer by playing it. Others, who have domestic obligations or don't care to push themselves to their limits, pick and choose their tournaments and spend the intervening times with their families or working on other jobs.

The itinerary can be grueling, but for the most part it is quite pleasant. It usually starts in Florida, then moves on to other Southern states like North Carolina,

Louisiana, Texas, Missouri and Kentucky. Then, as the North becomes warm enough to play in, the tour moves along to Wisconsin, Illinois, Ohio, Massachusetts, Canada, Michigan and back into the Midwest and South.

I was concerned that the appearance of a Negro on some of the courses might provoke incidents. I anticipated that some clubs would graciously accept my presence but feared that others would oppose it strenuously. Furthermore, there are a number of invitationals on the circuit. In an open tournament, any qualified pro or fee-paying amateur can play, at least theoretically (though if an open is held at a private instead of a public course, the club directors can try to bar an undesirable player). But most invitationals do not have requirements as to who *must* be invited— only who *may* be invited. A few invitationals require that the top-ranking ten or fifteen players, say, have to be invited, but in most cases there is no rule stating on what grounds the invitors invite the invitees.

Thus, even if my golf game merited invitations, the color of my skin might prevent some clubs from extending them to me.

As I suggested before, the possession of a player's card would at least give me some leverage against official discrimination on the tour, because an incident involving me would by association involve the L.P.G.A organization, and I would be able to seek its assistance in combating prejudice. I had no banner to wave, believe me, and didn't regard the L.P.G.A. as a power group to be infiltrated for the purpose of securing sweeping improvements in race relations. It would have made me happy if such improvements were a by-product of the association's functions, but I had no illusions. It is an organization constituted primarily for regulation of the sport of golf and has no interest in crusading for any purpose but decent treatment of its members and observance of official procedures by all parties. And that's how it should be.

I want to see the doors of all human endeavor thrown open to people of all races. But as I see it, the best way I can contribute to that purpose is to play my game as well as I can. Membership in the L.P.G.A. would at least give me a fair chance to do so, so it all came back to getting that card. If I sound as if I were slightly obsessed with it, you can see that it meant a good deal more to me than it might to a white player. It came, by and large, to be a comprehensive symbol of all I was striving for at that period in my life.

My playing improved considerably between 1963 and 1964, and it showed the effect of rigorous practice. I dropped my average from 84 to 77.5, and though this wasn't good enough to cop big prizes, I drew my first blood and finished the year with a total of $561.50 in winnings. When I compared that sum to the $29,800 that Mickey Wright won that year, I felt a little silly, but I was nevertheless immensely proud, just as I'm sure she was when she brought home her first paychecks.

And though I never won, placed or showed in a tournament that year, I still finished far enough ahead of the pack in enough tournaments to—you guessed it—earn my player's card. The receipt of it was one of the highlights of my career, marking a level of accomplishment I hadn't reached in about five years. I felt as if I'd just been handed a second birth certificate.

My satisfaction was made even keener by the circumstances in which I won it. The country club where one of the tournaments was held had permitted me to play on its course but requested that I refrain from using its clubhouse facilities. Having experienced this kind of silliness in the past, I accepted their treatment with half-amused resignation. The publicity that attends such incidents reflects to the club's detriment, not to mine, and I tried to be magnanimous whenever I was the victim. As long as I was allowed to play on the grounds, the use of the facilities was secondary.

By the time the tour got to this particular club, I needed a good score in just one more match in order to merit my player's card. By a delicious irony, it was at this very club that the feat was accomplished. Un-showered I may have been when I left that place, but I was so enthralled with my triumph that I just didn't care a hang.

I'm not a vengeful person, but in the face of unchari-table deeds few people can help hoping that their day will come. I wanted to climb to a position from which I could deal with such petty people on my own terms, not on theirs. I probably wouldn't do anything vin-dictive, any more than I had when I became tennis champion, but the satisfaction would come simply from being in that position.

The irony of this incident didn't end with the be-stowal on me of my player's card, however. The follow-ing year, whether because of me or because of some totally unrelated episode, the tournament was removed from that club and played at another in the same city. I like to give the benefit of the doubt to the forces of good and say that the shift was a form of retribution by a higher power. A somewhat similar incident occurred in another city. I was not permitted use of the club-house facilities at a certain club there, and the follow-ing year, on my way to another tournament, I passed through that city and asked the tournament sponsors if they would continue excluding me from full privi-leges. They told me in so many words that I still would not be welcome there, so I decided to pass up the tournament. But this time I had some leverage, being a full-fledged L.P.G.A. member, and I complained. And whether it was by virtue of my complaint or of something completely unassociated with the club's treatment of me, the tournament hasn't been held in that city since then.

I'm not gloating over these developments. No matter how much we like to think that human folly ought to be punished, I don't believe many of us feel unalloyed glee over the misfortunes of fools, no matter how much they deserve it. Still in all, if they bring it on themselves and we have been victimized by them, who is to blame us for feeling just a little pleasure to see justice being done.

There were some ugly scenes elsewhere, too, and I dealt with them as patiently as I could. My fellow players were sympathetic, but I couldn't ask them to jeopardize their positions to help me combat prejudice. I was satisfied simply knowing that they were there, however silently, on my side.

But if we bore these indignities quietly, there was someone not content to remain passive about them. This was Leonard Wirtz, tournament director of the United States Ladies' Professional Golf Association.

Lenny is a wonderful gentleman. A recent *Esquire* magazine article described his job as that of "social arbiter, fashion consultant, father substitute, and communal escort for thirty-five [the average number of L.P.G.A. girls who play in a tournament] nervous stomachs trying to become ulcers, six of which have already made it." When our tour came to one city, the owners of the private club holding the match there said I would not be permitted to play. Lenny, who had been growing more and more indignant over this kind of treatment, finally boiled over. He told the club that its opposition to me was in contradiction to the bylaws of the L.P.G.A., and he demanded that they let me play. They refused to relent, and Lenny therefore had the tournament withdrawn from the private club and moved to a public one.

The L.P.G.A. is at a disadvantage because in magnitude of prize money and publicity it is far inferior to the men's circuit. While such an episode on the men's tour would bring enormous public wrath upon the club owners, we had no such support on our humble little tour. Nevertheless gallant Lenny Wirtz, five foot five, snatched Princess Althea, five ten and a half, from the teeth of the dragon and has my eternal gratitude for his moving display of courage.

My biggest thrill in 1964 came in the opening round of the Thunderbird Open in Phoenix, Arizona. There I broke 70, shooting a 69 to take the lead. But the first day's success must have gone, quite literally, to my head because the next day I turned in an incorrect scorecard and was, by the severe but fair rules of the tour, disqualified from the tournament. It was little consolation the next year to see Doug Sanders, leading the pack in a major tournament, disqualified for the same reason. I was bitter with myself for such foolishness, but I learned a lesson. Now, every once in a while, instead of practicing on the putting greens after a match, I'll take a pencil and paper and practice my arithmetic. I've become so proficient I sometimes think that if I never reach the top in golf, I can always begin a career in mathematics.

Albert Einstein, move over!

11

Challenging Again

I WAS quite delighted with my progress in 1964. But satisfaction with past achievements doesn't entitle you to a free ride, as I'd painfully found out. So I decided to turn the heat up on myself, raising both the degree of difficulty and the output necessary to attain it. I practiced more rigorously than ever that winter, and by the time March of 1965 rolled around, I was in prime condition. I hoped to enter all important tournaments on the tour, this being the first year in which I'd be involving myself in the circuit up to the hilt.

I knew there would be the old problem of racial exclusion to tilt with, but I was unafraid. I had had enough combat duty in that theater to know that the best strategy is simply to be a winner. The world loves a winner and, though it may not be totally to humanity's credit, will champion a winner's cause while frequently ignoring the same cause advocated by some lesser light. You have to earn the world's respect and even wrest it out of its hands sometimes. I don't make up the rules; I just try to observe them.

But if the color of my skin was of secondary importance, the color of my bankbook was primary. By the beginning of 1965 it had the same drab appearance as the trees still cowering from winter cold. Looking ahead, I hoped to see green in my pocketbook as much as I did green on the trees. But I could count on the latter with more assurance.

Springtime had, for five years, always meant the renewal of my contract with Ward Baking. Since 1960 it had paid me a good salary which, though it decreased from year to year as I became less and less able to devote my undivided attention to serving them, enabled me to repay most of my debts. My relations with the company had continued to be among the most cordial of any I'd ever known. But it became obvious that the conflict between the demands their services made on me and those of my golf career would eventuate a decision. The Ward job wasn't the kind of figurehead position that would enable me to get away with posing for some publicity pictures once or twice a year and nothing more. It required my personal presence at and participation in a wide range of functions.

I wanted to stay with Ward but didn't see how I could fulfill my duties, so many of which took me far away from the cities on the golf tour. And looking at it from the other viewpoint, I might be critically knocked out of my golf groove by having to engage in activities for Tip-Top Bread. Thus when our contractual talks opened, I could see that something would have to give somewhere. I was hoping that my golf career would be an exciting one to my employers, and to an extent it was. But much as they were genuinely eager to see me rise to the top, I was not on top then. They may have felt, too, that the image of a championship golfer was not as compelling to buyers of their bread as that of a championship tennis player. And since I was an *ex*-champion tennis player and not yet a champion in golf, I imagine my image fell between two stools as far as their promotional campaigns were concerned.

Thus, to everyone's sorrow, a five-year relationship was brought to a close. Nobody could come up with a way to work out my schedule or duties to satisfy all parties. For the first time since 1960, I walked out of Ward's offices unfortified by the weight of a signed contract in my purse.

It was very depressing. Yet it was the natural consequence of my decision to be a golfer. Once you've committed yourself to a decision, you have to accept the penalties as well as reap the rewards.

I was a bit panicky as I realized I didn't have a single source of funds. I wanted to think I might count on some tournament purses, but until you're a consistent winner and can rely on a minimum number of victories per year to see you through, it's unwise, if not downright crazy, to count on anything. Besides, I needed money just to *join* the tour. Walking around Florida's golf courses is a pleasure, but walking *to* them from New York has very limited appeal to me. I needed to raise cash just to sustain me on the circuit, for even if I kept my belt tight and doubled up on room accommodations with some girls on the tour, I still would need between $750 and $1,000 a month for expenses. So I needed an outside source of income; if I won I'd be that much better off, but if I lost at least I wouldn't be worse off.

Luckily I was able to find a source that would lend me enough money to carry me through the season. It was a gratifying boost, relieving me of a bone-wearying burden and releasing me to devote my fullest attentions to my game. I budgeted myself as carefully as I'd done as an amateur tennis player. None of the borrowed money was earmarked for furs, pheasant under glass, or flashy jewelry. It went for basics, food and shelter, and even those were treated with austerity.

If anyone expected me to jump into the headlines—

and the high tax brackets—in 1965, I'm afraid I disappointed them. But from my standpoint, progress was considerable. I continued to lower my average and raise my winnings. But my official earnings for the year were $1,595.00, hardly what you would call a windfall. Yet it was a thousand dollars more than I'd won the previous year, and that evidently impressed my friends at the bank. They let me borrow again in 1966, and I'm pleased to say I think their risk was justified. For 1966 was the year of my Great Leap Forward. My average dropped to 74, a dip of ten strokes under my 1963 average, and my winnings rose to $3,221.50.

The biggest excitement of 1966 came for me on August 6, when in the Lady Carling Eastern Open, held at my favorite course, the Pleasant Valley Country Club in Sutton, Massachusetts, I broke the course record with a 68.

So far this year, 1967, I'm very happy about the way I've been playing. After knocking the rust out of my hinges in the opening match in St. Petersburg, I tied for fifth place in the next one, the Venice Ladies' Open, jumping from fourteenth position in the next-to-last round to fifth place with a 68 in the last round. That triumph alone brought in $572.00.

In May all thoughts of golf victories fled when I was informed that my father, who had ailed on and off for some time but who had been in good health lately, had suddenly—but, I am thankful, quietly—passed away. It came as a terrible shock to me. You think about these things, but you're never prepared for the reality when it comes. It left me deeply, infinitely sad. I can only console myself with the realization that he lived long enough to see me make something out of myself and to receive a few of the humble benefits of my success. Not all success stories in America are of the rags-to-riches kind, and if a man starts in rags and ends up with a little land, a nice house, the love of his children and all of his dignity, I think he can pass out of this world knowing he hasn't lived in vain.

12

The Challenges Ahead

AS I write this, I stand with one foot over the threshold of my fortieth year. That's a milestone in anyone's life, particularly a woman's, and especially in the life of a woman athlete. After all, there is hardly a difference between the way housework taxes a twenty-year-old woman and a forty-year-old one or the way business tasks tax a twenty-year-old lady executive or a forty-year-old one. In fact, if the physical strain gets to be too much for housewives or businesswomen as they age, they at least may have an opportunity to hire assistants.

But no athlete, man or woman, can be expected to keep up a twenty-year-old's pace at thirty-five, and at forty we look back at some of the feats we performed fifteen or twenty years earlier and wonder how on earth we managed half of them. Bear in mind, too, that an athlete can't hire someone to do his job.

So at the age of forty a woman athlete begins reviewing seriously the physical trials confronting her and the physical equipment she possesses to meet them. Some sports, like tennis, sprinting, baseball, football and boxing definitely belong to the young. These athletes have their peak years, some sooner and some later, but almost all sometime in their thirties, when their speed, agility, and reflexes begin declining. The decline doesn't have to be marked, but in national and international competition the slightest lapse makes an infinite amount of difference. By increasing his effort and compensating in other ways, the athlete can for a while make up for the losses, but the day must come when he realizes that his job or title are in jeopardy. He must then make a decision as to whether he will retire gracefully or lose his position in the violent way that many athletes do—a knockout, a disabling injury, a trade-off to another team, or a forced retirement.

I said a moment ago that athletes can't hire people to do their jobs, but that's not strictly true. An athlete can become a coach, manager or promoter and apply to the athletes he governs or handles the same principles and style that made him great. In that way the name and fame and even the technique of an athlete can be extended beyond his retirement, can even be immortalized, by the tradition he passes on to younger generations. And many athletes, examining their future during their prime years, determine on such careers and bring great honor to the sports world as directors or business executives.

If I've given the impression that an aging athlete has nothing to look forward to but the disintegration of his powers, however, let me hasten to correct it. It's certainly true that some functions diminish with age, but on the other side of the coin, as I've said, is the fact that others increase with increased years. And some don't even reach fruition until later in life. If an athlete loves challenge as much as I do and isn't prepared to withdraw entirely from active sports participation, he will assess his life in terms of improved abilities and capacities as well as in terms of slowing powers. He can look to those activities that aren't dominated by youth. Sports like bowling, golf and sailing, for example, not only aren't dependent on youth but actually favor age in the demands they make on one.

And finally, there are other careers and competitive activities that can absorb an athlete's instinct for challenge without making him feel he's been put out to pasture. I don't pretend to be an expert in psychology, but I do know that the athletic mentality can be satisfied vicariously by nonathletic occupations and pastimes, not empty, time-marking or time-killing ones but full-blown involvements. A business, a hobby, an entertainment career, and most certainly a marriage and family can keep a retired athlete deeply committed to life's challenges.

Clearly then, as I survey the future I see that whatever limitations my age places on it are amply balanced by the limitations my age removes. I'm freer, readier, more able and more eager to do some things than I ever was before. All it takes really is the courage to adapt myself to new conditions, and if I've ever been accused of shortcomings, inflexibility is not one of them.

I've spoken of golf as my new career, and until events overwhelmingly prove me wrong I intend to plug away at it with my eye fixed firmly on the big titles and the big purses. But once again, as in 1958, I've got irons in the fire, and if I fail in my bid for golf supremacy I'll by no means feel bereft.

Always in mind, sometimes in the back of it and sometimes in front but never out of consciousness entirely, is my dream of starting a sports academy. I believe the need for something like it is more pressing than ever before. Almost every traditional American and international sport has, in the last decade or two, reached unprecedented levels of professionalism. The finding and training of ambitious youngsters for these sports must be professionalized, too. We read of the old days when some rube walked into a baseball training camp, asked for a job and became one of the natural wonders of the game, or how some punk kid fighting in the streets was discovered by a boxing promoter and raised to become a champion. But with few exceptions such stories belong to a glamorous yesteryear. There are now a number of systems by which a child can make his way up into professional athletic ranks— Little Leagues, Golden Gloves, high school and college athletic programs and the like. But these systems incline to favor the privileged youngster, while the underprivileged is neglected or excluded because of his ignorance of the systems by which he can make his way to the top.

At this weak spot, then, I would establish my academy, serving a number of important functions. It would try to locate talented but impecunious youngsters or try through the slum grapevine to make its facilities known to them, much as Police Athletic Leagues do. It would train those youths, eliminating bad habits and developing their strengths and natural capacities. It would also tutor them in sports rules, hygiene, sportsmanlike conduct and the economics of amateur and professional athletics. It would act as informal liaison between athletes and sports scouts, bringing the youths' virtues to the attention of coaches and managers. It might act as friend in court, advising youngsters on college scholarships or helping them negotiate professional contracts.

Ideally, I would like to subsidize this nonprofit academy with my own funds, but perhaps the community might contribute, either informally or officially through government help. Perhaps the youths themselves would assist financially. If we gave an athlete a big enough push, he might one day return the favor with a modest endowment. Or if we arranged an impressive contract for a youngster, he might offer us some small portion to help us perpetuate our services so that others like him might be similarly helped. Needless to say, such contributions would be voluntary, and we would refuse money if it appeared to strap the benefactor. Government help is a much more promising answer, and current administrators of poverty programs might see my academy as an effective way to utilize some of their budget.

This plan represents my ideal of public service, but I still nurture hopes of private fulfillment as well. If my academy never comes to fruition—and I'm aware of the many factors militating against it—there are alternate courses which could prove just as gratifying, if not more so, and other ways in which I can make a public contribution while meeting my private demands at the same time.

150

Some time ago I made the acquaintance of Nat Sackin, a talent and business manager for a number of sports and entertainment figures. Nat had been owner of the Bonsoir nightclub on West Eighth Street in Greenwich Village, a spot where many singers and comedians who are now the biggest in the business were launched or helped along. Woody Allen, Barbra Streisand and Phyllis Diller were given considerable impetus by Nat's shrewd promotion, and in the early 1960's the Bonsoir was one of the hottest spots in New York. After Nat left the Bonsoir, he went full time into the talent-management business, and he has worked with such artists as Ella Fitzgerald, Eartha Kitt and Roy Hamilton.

As I just said, the last few decades have seen sports take on a new luster of professionalism, and many athletes have lawyers, business or career managers, or talent agents to assist them not only in getting good terms on their sports contracts but in securing and negotiating nonsport contracts such as commercials and endorsements, lectures and other personal appearances. My mind had been dwelling on the idea of engaging such a manager in the early sixties, but of course I have now an additional reason for seeking one, namely my singing career. If you think I've let that one go to seed, you're very much mistaken. Though I haven't been cultivating my singing in a disciplined way in the last few years, I've still kept up my practicing whenever I can. In fact, I believe that my voice has taken on depth in the last few years and is more mellow and expressive than ever before.

When I told Nat about myself on the occasion of our first meeting, he asked me if I'd really been organizing my time, talents and ambitions for maximum impact. I saw that there was room for improvement. We decided to review them all in order to determine a more systematic approach, to say nothing of a more profitable one. And so Nat and I joined forces, and he has been enormously helpful to me in regularizing my business affairs and cultivating my talents. Nat's experience with singing stars along with that of his associate, Sammy Benskin, has enabled him to detect flaws in my delivery and rectify them, so that I'm now picking songs best suited to my vocal range and using that range for maximum effectiveness.

So my self-confidence as a singer has been amply restored, and I'm now casting an eye once more on nightclub and television appearances and thinking about cutting another record, this time under more agreeable circumstances. I mentioned some time back that in 1943 I won second place in the amateur-night competition at Harlem's Apollo Theater. That entitled me to a week's engagement there, but for twenty-five years I've been waiting in vain for the invitation.

I think I've given the Apollo managers enough time to find a spot for me on their schedule. So Bobby Schiffman, Honi Cole, and Peter Long—be advised.

They say a performer is married to her manager, and in many ways the ties between client and manager are as strong as, if not stronger than, those between husband and wife. But as fond as I am of Nat Sackin, and as great a help to me as he has been, my "marriage" with him can't compare to the profound fulfillment I've found in my marriage—my real marriage to Will Darben. Didn't I mention it? I guess I was saving the best till last.

I suppose Will must think of me the way I think of that Apollo appearance—it took me twelve years to get around to making my return engagement. You'll remember that he proposed to me in 1953, but so much stood in our way that I had to refuse him and place our relationship on a strictly friendship level. But in the decade that followed, we had grown up and grown together, and by 1963 he felt another assault on my armor would not go unrequited. But I was still resisting, though for the life of me I can't think of anything but sheer feminine perversity that kept me from accepting. I guess I just wanted to prove once more to him, to the world, and above all to myself that I am worthy of being loved and respected. And in 1964 on the golf links I did prove it, in spite of Will's protestations that if his love depended on my success, it would have all been over for us long ago.

And so as 1965 came and went, my love for Will grew beyond manageable proportions, and in October of that year we decided to stop fighting the inevitable. We agreed over the long-distance phone that he would join me in Las Vegas. There we were married in a quiet, dignified ceremony before Mr. and Mrs. Homer Devore. After a brief honeymoon we traveled to Phoenix, where I played in a tournament. Although Will had watched me play in many matches, I felt almost childishly nervous to know that my *husband* was in the gallery that day!

You would think that after knowing Will for over fifteen years I would have little to learn about him, but marriage has disclosed a world of endlessly fascinating discoveries. For instance, he'd told me he played the piano a bit, but I never imagined he indulged in this pastime with any seriousness. It came as a delightful shock to me to learn that he is not only quite accomplished at the piano but also has a talent for song composition. Since he's never had a piano of his own, I decided to give him one for a wedding present. Our leisure evenings together in our New Jersey home—the home he inherited from his mother —are frequently spent making music, literally.

Will is quite well involved in his position at Bendix

and so cannot accompany me on my tours. This is just as well for both of us, for Will has his own career to develop, and his income helps level off the ups and downs of my golfer's income. He is actually the bread-winner, and that's perfectly fine with me, liberating me as it does to play my game without feeling the pressure of making a living by it. On the other hand, some golf purses couldn't hurt. . . .

In addition, Will knows I might get nervous if he were out there in the crowd watching me. But separation from each other isn't as bad as we'd anticipated. We talk to each other constantly by phone, and I superstitiously carry our marriage license in my purse, with that player's card, at all times.

But even when he isn't by my side or encouraging me over the phone, the very certainty I have of his devotion inspires me to plug on in the face of discouragement and gives me someone to share the rewards with when I prevail. Above everything and everyone else, Will has given me reason to sing, with deeper feeling than ever before, my song, "So Much to Live For." For I am immensely committed to life now. I'm somebody both in my own eyes and someone else's, whatever I am to the world at large. But I'll still go on wanting to be somebody to the world at large, too.

We constantly tread the borders of discouragement,

and the devil perpetually whispers "Why don't you give up?" in our ears. But the person who lets go, whatever his role in life and whatever his age, will soon experience a decline in mental and physical well-being. Eternal challenge is life itself, and though it brings us sobbing to our knees, the glory of humanity is in the way it rises from heartbreaking setbacks to reach sublime heights of achievement. Even if that achievement is recognized by no one but yourself, you are nevertheless at one with the most celebrated of historical figures.

For when you weigh their final satisfaction beside your own, you realize there is no difference. The noblest and humblest stand equal under the banner that declares, simply and eloquently: WE TRIED.

Index

157

The Authors

ALTHEA GIBSON grew up in Harlem, where she learned to take care of herself, sometimes with her fists. From hanging around poolrooms and bowling alleys, somehow she gravitated to table tennis and then tennis. After capping her career as one of the world's outstanding champions at amateur tennis, she turned to the professional tennis court, and then to professional golf.

RICHARD CURTIS was born in The Bronx, and has spent most of his life in New York City. He was graduated from Syracuse University and earned his MA at the University of Wyoming. After working for a literary agency, he decided to turn to full-time freelance writing. He is the author of several articles and books. Mr. Curtis lives in Manhattan with his wife, Jeanne, who hails from St. Louis, Missouri.